OPEN MY EYES, OPEN MY SOUL

OPEN MY EYES, OPEN MY SOUL

Celebrating Our Common Humanity

Created by

Yolanda King
Elodia Tate

Foreword by Coretta Scott King

McGraw-Hill

New York   Chicago   San Francisco
Lisbon   London   Madrid   Mexico City
Milan   New Delhi   San Juan   Seoul

The **McGraw·Hill** Companies

4 5 6 7 8 9 0   AGM/AGM   0 9 8 7 6 5 4

ISBN 0-07-143886-6

"For Our World" from *Journey Through Heartsongs* by Mattie Stepanek. Copyright 2002 Mattie Stepanek. Reprinted with permission of Hyperion.

"Human Family" from *I Shall Not Be Moved* by Maya Angelou. Copyright © 1990 by Maya Angelou. Used by permission of Random House.

"The Artist in Us All" by Freddie Ravel originally appeared in *Hot Chocolate for the Mystical Soul,* 1998. Reprinted with permission of the author.

"Baby Flight" by Paul Karrer originally appeared in *A 4th Course of Chicken Soup for the Soul,* 1997. Reprinted with permission of the author.

"Amen, Indeed" by Karen Waldman originally appeared in *Chicken Soup for the Veteran's Soul,* 2000, as "Ebony & Ivory." Reprinted with permission of the author.

McGraw-Hill books are available at special discounts to use as premiums and sales promotions, or for use in corporate training programs. For more information, please write to the Director of Special Sales, Professional Publishing, McGraw-Hill, Two Penn Plaza, New York, NY 10121-2298. Or contact your local bookstore.

Library of Congress Cataloging-in-Publication Data

Open my eyes, open my soul : celebrating our common humanity / created by Yolanda King and Elodia Tate.
    p. cm.
  ISBN 0-07-143886-6 (pbk. : alk. paper)
  1. Pluralism (Social sciences)   2. Toleration.   3. Humanity.   I. King, Yolanda. II. Tate, Elodia.
  HM1271.O63 2004
  179'.9—dc22

2003023543

Dedicated to our human family,
and the realization that we are one.

CONTENTS

PART I: REALIZING OUR ONENESS

PART II: CELEBRATING DIVERSITY

PART III: ONE IN SPIRIT

PART IV: CHOSEN CHILDREN

PART V: LOVE BEYOND BOUNDARIES

Part VI: Creating the Beloved Community

FOREWORD

As a young mother some years ago, I welcomed every opportunity to teach my children as best I could about the wonder of human diversity, and it was gratifying to witness the expansion of their awareness of the contributions of all races, religions, and nations to the progress of humanity. My firstborn daughter, Yolanda, relished these insights with particular fervor and became increasingly devoted to using the arts and media to bring people together and to educate young people in particular about the empowering values of nonviolence and the benefits of greater intercultural understanding, goodwill, and cooperation.

Even in this age of increasingly sophisticated electronic media, spending some quiet time with a book that inspires and uplifts the human spirit remains one of the most fulfilling of life's pleasures. And this is what Yolanda and her cocreator, Elodia Tate, have produced with the publication of *Open My Eyes, Open My Soul*—a collection of stories and poems that speak to our deeply felt longing for a more loving and compassionate world community, with vivid, real life examples and eloquent explorations of the human imagination.

Open My Eyes, Open My Soul is a kind of spiritual travel guide that takes its readers on myriad journeys, deep into the hearts and souls of the wonderful, diverse human beings who populate these pages. These stories and poems illuminate the lives of people struggling to make meaningful connections by reaching out with courage and love across the chasms of race, religion, culture, boundaries, and other man-made barriers.

Although the voices in *Open My Eyes, Open My Soul* touch on many facets of the mirror ball of human experience, together they offer hope that there is an undercurrent of common consciousness that unites all of humanity in some mysterious and transcendent way, and every effort to promote greater sisterhood and brotherhood, no matter how small or large the scale may be, is worthy of celebration.

Read on, then, with confidence that this book is part of your unique journey to wholeness. Learn the empowering lessons of unconditional love, hope, and healing contained herein and know that you too have a vital contribution to make to the creation of the Beloved Community.

Coretta Scott King

Introduction

The creation of this book, from the very beginning, has been a divinely guided process for both of us. For Yolanda, it was an extension of the work that she has been doing, both on the stage as an actor and behind the podium as a speaker, to raise awareness about our oneness. For Elodia, the vision for the book was the result of being a part of a multicultural family and facing the issues of diversity. We came together to create a literary work that would encourage readers to recognize, accept, and celebrate our common humanity.

When we first met to discuss this idea for this book, it was clear to us that we shared a vision, a passion, and a purpose for bringing this message to others. It was a meeting of the hearts as well as the minds, and it was evident that we could blend both our strengths and our own unique talents into a vehicle that could facilitate this process. We have worked step by step and side by side, collaborating and both using our abilities to the fullest.

We love the written word, and the idea of an anthology appealed to us. Both of us know firsthand the power of a story or poem to communicate a message and to bring about self-examination of the soul. We knew that there had to be lots of wonderful stories out there that needed to be shared as a way of illuminating the path for ourselves and others.

Our first step toward collecting the material needed was to get the word out to others. This was the fun part. People would get so excited when we told them about our project. Even the people who didn't have a story would offer us their prayers and would support or contact others who did have a story to share. We would hear exclamations from the people we would speak to about this project, such as "The world needed this book yesterday!" or "Can you get me copies of that book tomorrow?" The enthusiasm was such that we knew this was not just a good idea but a "God" idea.

It was important for both of us to provide an outlet for young or "unpublished" writers. We encouraged this by staging a contest for the best contribution from an unpublished author. We took advantage of Yolanda's speaking opportunities and performances to tell others about our project. Yolanda handed out brochures by the thousands, and sometimes they were passed on to people so many times over that we could not locate the original source. We created a website that Elodia managed, and she used the internet to reach out to potential contributors. We invited people to send us their work, and the stories and poems starting flooding our mailboxes and e-mail folders. It was so amazing to see the responses from so many people, so quickly. Our website actually got overloaded and started returning submissions from people that were trying to submit their work to us prior to our deadline. This was a good problem to have. In fact, we had such an overwhelming response that we had to extend our deadline, which we did again and again, to give opportunity to all of those working hard to make our final selections.

The contributions we received have come from all over the world, from places such as Japan, the Philippines, the Netherlands, Switzerland, Colombia, South Africa, and all of the United States. The submissions came from people of all ages, races, and genders, including children.

Our contributors have been so gracious. They write us the most heartfelt letters telling us that they are honored we are reading their work. So many people write to us "thanking" us for doing this project. We also hear from our contributors that even if their piece was not accepted, they appreciate being a part of the process. Several people even wrote just to wish us well.

We have developed deep friendships with our contributors. We get invitations to visit them or go hiking and sight-seeing. Many people write offering to open their homes to us when we go on book tours, and to let us enjoy a home-cooked meal with them and a place to stay if need be. The love and the outpouring of support from our contributors has been so amazing that it serves as evidence of the connectedness we all share. Our lives have been enormously enriched.

Each story or poem in this book was included because it contained a unique element and we felt each one needed to be part of this collection. The people who wrote these stories bared their souls, and some shared with us their most significant life events, which have shaped or changed their perspectives. We learned from our writers, and as we read these special works, we experienced laughter and shed many tears. This process has also included reading selections out loud in groups. Somehow the spoken word brings to life the spirit of the message.

For the selection process, we had a fabulous and diverse group of readers, who were so dedicated to reading and rating each contribution. Our group included men, women, and children from various backgrounds and cultures. It is interesting for us to read all of the ratings, and compare how a certain story affected the readers. All of the contributions chosen from our selection process were rated as tens, from a scale of one through ten. We asked our readers to rate each item based on the statements that applied such as "This item moved me emotionally, made me laugh, made me cry, gave me a new insight, had me stop to reflect on the message given, changed a perspective of mine, made me want to share it with others, made me more aware of situations I didn't know existed, taught me about a culture I knew little about, made me feel more connected to others, made me more aware of my thoughts or actions toward others, and made me want to change something about myself for the better." When the surveys were returned, it was clear to us which selections were best suited for our book.

There are certain stories or poems that, when we say the title, a smile crosses our face and we blurt out "I love that story." Sometimes we say a name of a title like "The Baby Flight" or "Almost Sisters," and everyone sighs and repeats the title in unison. Then there are the stories that have affected some of our readers so much on an emotional level that it motivated them to write a story of their own. Two of the stories we have in this book actually came from two of our readers, "Guardian Angel" and "Two Cultures, One World, One Humanity." No, they didn't get to rate their own stories, and the other readers also didn't know they wrote them. In fact, our authors' names were kept secret during the rating process.

The final selections went through additional rounds of voting, and it was difficult because there were so many inspirational stories that we could not include for one reason or another, but we love and feel connected to them all.

After we made the final selections, it was time to announce our finalist for our unpublished author contest. We had five finalists, and those we were able to reach by phone would shriek and laugh and yell and be so thrilled to get a call from us, which would thrill us in return. We held an online vote placing their stories or poems on our website, and invited others to vote for their favorite selection. We had hundreds of votes come in, and all of the votes were close, with the exception of our winning title "Danny" written by Abby Warmuth. She won the contest hands down!

We put much thought into every element of the book. Even the naming of the sections was done with special consideration. The contents of each chapter was carefully selected, and even the celebrity contributions were chosen for a particular element we felt that individual could contribute.

During the process of creating this work, the hand of divine guidance continued to nudge us with a stream of "coincidences." It seemed that we would just speak an idea or make a suggestion to one another, and the phone would ring the next day with someone offering to fulfill that newly voiced request. Those events served as a constant reminder that we were on the right path.

As an example of how the doors have been opened by a power much higher than our own, let us share with you this quick story. We had a poem we wanted to include titled "Underneath We Are All The Same." This poem had been in Yolanda's possession for years, and we felt its words resonated so well with our message. The young lady who wrote the poem was only fifteen years old at the time. That was over eight years ago. The only information we had was her name, Amy Maddox, and the name of the high school she had attended. We called the school, hoping by chance they might be able to help us. When we told the woman on the other end of the line why we were calling, there was dead silence for a moment. Then she replied "You're not going to believe this, but I am holding in my hand the transcripts for Amy Maddox. Her college requested them, and her name is now Amy Skirvin." Then she gave us the phone number, and we were able to connect with that author.

On another occasion, we needed to obtain the approval for a poem we wanted to use titled "For Our World," from child poet and hero Mattie Stepanek. We were having difficulty getting to the right person at his publisher's office and could find no other way to contact him. Then Elodia's daughter, Dionne, received an invitation to attend a poetry convention in Washington, D.C., to accept a poetry award. When the itinerary came up, it stated that a featured speaker of the event was Mattie Stepanek. Mattie's health is compromised as he deals with a form of muscular dystrophy. We kept it in our prayers that he would be well enough to attend this event and that we would be able to speak to him. As it turned out, both Elodia and her daughter did get to speak to Mattie and his mother. Mattie had been in the hospital for five months and was just released in time to attend this event. Mattie and his mother had heard about our project and were very honored and excited to offer Mattie's poem as a contribution. In turn, we were honored to meet Mattie as well. To top it off, we now have autographed books and photos with our new friend. Stay well, Mattie.

Prior to that same Washington, D.C., trip and feeling that we now had a good handle on our manuscript, we wanted the advice of a literary agent. The day before Elodia was to leave, she corresponded by e-mail to literary agent Jeff Kleinman. She had no idea where Jeff was located. Jeff suggested they meet and discuss the possibility of this book. When she e-mailed him back and told him that would not be possible because she was leaving the next day for Washington, D.C., he e-mailed back "Where in D.C.?" She told him the name of the hotel where she and her daughter would be staying, and he replied that his office was just across the street from that hotel. In fact, he was looking at the hotel from his window.

The meeting was successful and initiated the process of obtaining a publishing contract.

We were so fortunate that our publisher was willing to work within our time frame of getting this book released for the King Holiday 2004. In fact, people told us it would be a miracle to accomplish getting this book done so quickly. Well, our miracle arrived because the staff at McGraw-Hill and our agent have been amazing and have done everything in their power to work with our vision and to make this book become a reality for all of us.

We are thrilled and humbled to have been a part of this project: it's been an extraordinary experience to connect with all of the people who have made it possible—and most of all, to have the possibility of connecting with you as you journey through *Open My Eyes, Open My Soul*. We hope that you too will experience the kind of awakening that we, and the writers in this collection, all shared: our feeling that new possibilities suddenly sprang open before us. We hope this book will take you to new places in your soul—and that you'll pass these pages along to someone else, so that he or she, too, can share in these writers' unique visions.

Throughout our process, we've been inspired by a Hasidic tale Rev. Ron Fox shared with us:

> A rabbi asks his students, "How can we tell when night has passed?" One student says, "When it is possible to tell a dog from a wolf." Another responds,

"When it is possible to identify the fruit on a tree." As each student responds, the rabbi shakes his head, no. Finally, one student cries out in frustration, "Then you tell us!" The rabbi smiles and says, "It is when you can look on the face of any man or woman and see it is your brother or sister. Because if you cannot see this, it is still night."

Together, we enrich each other. It's as if we are following a road we've walked down a hundred times before, when suddenly one of us sees a path we'd never noticed before branching off into the underbrush; and, together, we take it, and follow it, and find a horizon that we couldn't have imagined, a vista that leaves us breathless and delighted and—in the end—thankful to be alive.

Join us as we move from the night into the sunlight of acceptance.

Yolanda King
Elodia Tate

PART I

REALIZING OUR ONENESS

We are caught in an inescapable network of mutuality, clothed in a single garment of destiny. Whatever affects one directly affects all indirectly. I can never be what I ought to be until you are what you ought to be, and you can never be what you ought to be until I am what I ought to be. This is the interrelated structure of reality.

—Martin Luther King, Jr.

HUMAN FAMILY

Maya Angelou

I note the obvious differences
in the human family.
Some of us are serious,
some thrive on comedy.

Some declare their lives are lived
as true profundity,
and others claim they really live
the real reality.

The variety of our skin tones
can confuse, bemuse, delight,
brown and pink and beige and purple,
tan and blue and white.

I've sailed upon the seven seas
and stopped in every land,
I've seen the wonders of the world
not yet one common man.

I know ten thousand women
called Jane and Mary Jane,

but I've not seen any two
who really were the same.

Mirror twins are different
Although their features jibe,
and lovers think quite different thoughts
while lying side by side.

We love and lose in China,
we weep on England's moors,
and laugh and moan in Guinea,
and thrive on Spanish shores.

We seek success in Finland,
are born and die in Maine.
In minor ways we differ,
in major we're the same.

I note the obvious differences
between each sort and type,
but we are more alike, my friends,
than we are unalike.

We are more alike, my friends,
than we are unalike.

We are more alike, my friends,
than we are unalike.

THE LAND WE SHARE

Robert F. Kennedy, Jr.

My mother said it happened while I was in my crib—my love for nature, that is. She said I was always fascinated with every living creature I came in contact with. It started with the little bugs I would find and then moved on to larger animals like pigeons, hawks, and horses. I think it must be coded in my DNA somehow because I can't ever remember not being in awe of the living creatures of this planet, and I grew up thinking I would be a veterinarian one day.

I can remember visiting my uncle, President Kennedy, when I was a little boy with my father and eight or nine of my brothers and sisters. We would go to the Justice Department and visit about twice a week for lunch. I would look up at the old post office building and see a bird that was a type of ferruginous hawk that would nest there. This particular type of ferruginous hawk was salmon pink with a white coverlet, and I thought they were the most beautiful birds I had ever seen. I would watch these birds, who could fly over two hundred miles an hour. They would fly at those speeds and pick pigeons out of the sky that were only forty feet above our heads. To me, watching that site was even more exciting than visiting my uncle at the White House.

My father took me mountain climbing and white water rafting, and we would visit the wonderful national parks and forests of this country. It was my experience with the natural environment that first helped me to begin to understand our oneness as humanity. I was taught that we share these lands in common with others and that it was our responsibility to protect our common lands and the resources such as the air, the water, the wandering animals, and the fisheries. The legal scholars of all ages have believed there is a natural law that requires the community to protect the land. That is what our first early American settlers believed and practiced. In ancient Rome protection of the dunelands and wetlands was long-established law.

I was only fourteen when my father, Senator Robert Kennedy, Sr., was killed. However, I made a decision to follow in my father's footsteps and do my best to continue his fight. My father fought for basic human rights for all people, regardless of race, religion, or economic backgrounds. He didn't preach or lecture us, but he led by example, and those lessons stuck with me. I felt comfortable fighting for something I believed in, which is a basic right for all humans to breathe clean air and have clean water. I attended Harvard, just like my father, and then received a law degree from the University of Virginia Law School. I went on and became a prosecuting attorney, but felt like something was missing from my life. That was twenty years ago.

In 1983 I became the prosecuting attorney for an organization called the Riverkeepers. I identified with this group right away. These were hard-working people of military backgrounds, much like my own family.

The organization was started in the 1960s with blue-collar workers, commercial fishermen of the Hudson River. This was a patriotic group of people, not militants or radicals. They would meet in the American Legion Hall to discuss how they saw the fisheries being exploited.

The Hudson River was once condemned as an open sewer in the 1960s. Today it is regarded as one of the richest water bodies on earth. The river produces more fish per acre and more biomass per gallon that any other river on the North Atlantic coast. It is now an international model inspired by the creation of the Riverkeepers, and programs are starting from the East Coast to the West Coast. We are even starting in Australia and other places around the globe.

I enjoy being with the fishermen, and hanging out with wildlife on the river, but our work is far from over. Our statistics today read like a science fiction nightmare. Four out of five dumps or waste sites are near housing in African-American neighborhoods, like the south side of Chicago or areas in east Los Angeles. Our Navajo youth are seventeen times more likely than others to get cancer in their sexual organs, because of the toxicity of their land. Did you know it is illegal to eat fresh fish caught in the state of Connecticut owing to the high mercury contamination? Did you know that in China they now have oxygen bars where you can buy clean air to breathe?

One in four children born in a city in the United States have asthma, and that includes my own children, who suffer from asthma. Do you remember I mentioned how much I loved seeing the ferruginous hawks when I was a boy? Well, that is a sight that my children will never get to see because that species of bird became extinct in 1963, because of DDT poisoning.

No matter what our race, creed, or color is, no matter where we live or how much money we have, we all share one thing in common, and that is the land. We all need clean air to breathe, and fresh water to drink. This one issue connects us more profoundly than any other challenge that we face. It is my hope that we can work together to build a world community that allows us these basic human rights.

Through a Child's Eyes

Marie McBride

On my way to work each morning, I stop by a local restaurant for breakfast and to read the newspaper.

One morning I noticed an adorable African-American child sitting alone at a table beside the service counter. She had her coloring books, crayons and Barbie dolls in a small backpack on the seat beside her. For the next several days, I noticed her quietly playing with her toys and carefully watching a young woman behind the counter.

After a week of exchanging smiles with this darling child, I asked if I could sit with her for a moment. She answered, "Yes." She pointed to the woman working behind the counter and added, "That's mama. I stay here 'til school starts." I walked to her mother and asked permission to eat with her daughter. Her mother agreed and added, "Yes, she gets bored waiting for the bus. I have to bring her to work with me at six o'clock because I don't have nowhere to leave her." Her mother told me she was a single mom and worked the morning shift so she could be home when Andrea got out of school.

That day, Andrea and I began a special friendship. She was three years old.

When I arrived at the restaurant at seven o'clock every morning, Andrea was waiting for me. She'd have my napkin, knife and straw on the table. While we ate breakfast, we colored pictures, played word games, and read books. After a few weeks, I asked her mother if she could ride with me to the post office to pick up the office mail. In less than a week, Andrea could find the post office box and open it. Every day she would put the mail in my briefcase and then hold this huge briefcase in her tiny hands and lug it to my car. She said, "I'm helping you, Marie." On my way to the office, I dropped her off at the restaurant to wait for her bus.

Andrea invited me to her fourth birthday party at a skating rink. I held her hand while she tried to skate and helped her mother serve birthday cake to the other children.

Our friendship grew. I took Andrea to plays, movies, concerts, museums, libraries. Each time I picked Andrea up at her house, she wore a frilly dress, matching tights and patent-leather shoes. Her mother would have her hair set in an elaborate style with dozens of colored beads, ribbons and barrettes. When I complimented Andrea on her beautiful hair, she said, "It hurts when mama combs it, and it takes a long time!"

One Saturday afternoon when Andrea was about six years old, we went to an ice cream store after a children's theater play. The mall was crowded and busy, and I held her hand tightly walking through the parking lot. She glanced at our hands several times, but said nothing. While we sat in the booth eating our ice cream cones, she asked, "Do you know you're white?"

"Yes," I answered, "Is that okay?" She rolled her eyes, paused a moment, then said, "It's just skin." For two years, she hadn't noticed that we were different—that I was white and she was black. All she knew was that I loved her.

Over the next eleven years we spent many happy times together. Sometimes I invited her mother to join us for dinner, but Andrea said, "I like it better when it's just us!"

When she was fourteen years old, she and her mother moved out of state to care for her ill grandfather. We all cried when we said good-bye and promised that we would never forget one another. In my heart, I know we've kept that promise.

THE GIFT WE ARE

Caroline Castle Hicks

We come into the world wrapped up only in skin;
it's a wonderful way for us all to begin.

For we're wrapped up in colors more lovely by far
than the paper and ribbon on any gift are.

We come wrapped up in shades; some are dark, some are light,
like a beach in the morning, like a deep, star-filled night.

We come wrapped in the colors of the fields, hills and skies,
from the brown of our hair to the blue of our eyes.

We come wrapped up in colors, red, yellow and brown,
like the quiet fall woods with the leaves coming down.

We come wrapped up in all kinds of beautiful colors;
we come wrapped in the arms of the people who love us.

But what matters the most from the day we begin,
is the gift that we are, and it comes from within.

GUARDIAN ANGEL
Adoralida (Dora) Padilla

In the fall of 1998, my friend Eleanor, a seasoned traveler, wanted to visit Turkey but couldn't find anyone to join her. I had always wanted to travel, and figured I had to start somewhere, so I signed on for a five-week trip.

We arrived in Istanbul. This was such an ancient city: Constantinople, Byzantium, the center of the Roman Empire; we were truly in awe and very humbled. The Haiga Sophia, the Blue Mosque, the Grand Bazaar—we saw it all.

We decided to venture out from Istanbul heading toward Izmir by ferry. Then, we would take a train to Selcuk where we would be only minutes away from the ancient ruins of Ephesus. Arriving at the ferry office rather early, we were the first ones there, other than a scruffy homeless-looking Turk asleep on a bench. We sat as far away from him as we could. His shoes were several sizes too big, and the soles were flopping off. His socks had been worn through at the heel, and turned so now the hole was at the front ankle. His pants were baggy and dirty, his jacket had holes, and he was in serious need of a shower and a shave.

People started to filter into the ferry building, getting in line to buy their tickets. Although most of the people we encountered spoke English, the ticket seller did not. It was difficult to convey that we wanted both ferry tickets and train tickets. To my surprise, the homeless-looking man appeared at my side, and in near perfect English told us that we were in the wrong line. He guided us to the proper line, ordered our tickets, made sure I counted my currency correctly and that I received the proper change. He told me his name was Sinan.

Sinan helped us with our very heavy bags onto the ferry, and up several flights of stairs to the top observation deck. The seats were full. He asked a family at a nice booth to please let us sit there, and they obliged. We invited him to sit with us, and offered to buy him breakfast for all his help. He only accepted a cup of coffee.

Sinan explained he was in Istanbul for a job interview with a cruise line. He had worked at major hotels in Saudi Arabia and London. From his torn jacket, he produced his prized possession—a Polaroid picture of himself with Sean Connery, taken in London. He accompanied us out onto the deck and told us all about the sites along the Bosporus. We spent hours on the ferry enjoying his company, and took Polaroid pictures of ourselves with him. He placed our picture together with the picture of Sean Connery.

When we arrived at our stop, Sinan didn't even hesitate before grabbing our bags and carrying them down the stairs. After walking us to the train station, he quickly paid a porter to watch our bags, and we walked several blocks to a pizzeria for lunch. We insisted on buying lunch, but he ate very little. He carried our bags onto the train, and again asked people to move so we had perfect seats. We didn't realize the ferry trip would be about three hours and the train trip another eight hours. While Eleanor napped, Sinan and I talked about every subject under the sun: politics, the role of women in Turkish society, religion, family, law, UFO's (he was convinced, as he said many Turks were, that America had contact with aliens and that is why we had advanced technology). He was bright, funny, insightful, naive.

We had not finished our lunch, and he had the foresight to have our leftovers wrapped up. We ate cold pizza and the people he had kicked out of our seats shared apples and bread with us. We told him where we were headed, and he asked where we planned to stay once we arrived in Selcuk. He advised that we should get off several stops before the end of the line, to be closer to the bus station where we had to connect to our final destination.

By the time we arrived in Izmir, it was about eleven p.m. Sinan helped us off the train, picked up our bags, one on each shoulder, and started off down a busy expressway. It was all Eleanor and I could do to keep up with him, in the dark. We feared we had made a terrible mistake, entrusting this stranger with our belongings, and that he was now running off with all we had. I saw him turn off way ahead, and Eleanor and I were out of breath trying to catch up. When we turned the same corner, we saw Sinan standing in front of a magnificent Mercedes bus, with our luggage in front of him, and his arms spread out wide to stop the bus which was pulling out of the station.

The driver got out and yelled at him, and he answered back in Turkish. The driver opened the storage area, and threw our bags in. We arrived breathless and Sinan ushered us onto the bus, telling us we could buy the tickets on board. He gave us a hurried hug good-bye, and he was drenched in sweat from running with our luggage. The moment we were on the bus, it pulled out of the station. Sinan ran alongside the bus, waving excitedly. It was then I noticed tears running down my face. I had missed the chance to tell my new friend how much we appreciated his kindness and company. We waved back and he was gone.

Eleanor and I sat and looked at each other and at the same time said: "He was a guardian angel!" Had it not been for Sinan, we would not have purchased the proper tickets, we would have labored terribly with our bags, we would have missed out on good seating, and who knows what we would have done about food. We would have missed the delightful guided tour of the Bosporus on the ferry. We would have gotten off at the wrong station, had to hire a taxi, and would have missed the last bus to Selcuk that night, leaving us stranded without reservations near midnight in a strange city.

When we arrived in Selcuk, it was nearly midnight. The little town was asleep. There was no one in sight. We were the only passengers getting off at that town. There was a man leaning by a car. He eyed us carefully. We were instantly worried. The man approached and asked: "Are you the American women coming from Istanbul?" We were shocked. "How did you know?" we asked. He answered: "Because a man named Sinan called the hotel and told us you would be arriving on this bus. He said you'd be hungry and asked that we keep the kitchen open for you." We couldn't believe it. Even though he was no longer traveling with us, Sinan, our guardian angel, was still looking out for us.

The man took our luggage and drove us the few blocks to our hotel. The kitchen was open and waiting to serve us dinner.

That night, as I drifted off to sleep, I felt ashamed for having initially judged Sinan by his appearance. I was also sad that such a wonderful man had so few opportunities—his greatest desire was to someday come to the United States and work at a 7-11 store. Most importantly, I was thankful to have opened my eyes to discover kindness when and where it was least expected.

It was stunning how much a total stranger was willing to do for us, without expecting anything in return. Throughout our adventure in Turkey, we saw this same kindness repeated time and time again. We never knew his last name, but we will always remember him as "Sinan, the guardian angel."

Understand Why

Bernie Siegel, M.D.

Many years ago my great grandfather told me of the persecution he experienced in Russia which led him to come to America. He said that when he was out teaching at night, the Cossacks would pursue him and slash him with their sabers. One night he was on the hill above his village with his rabbi, the Baal Shem Tov. As they looked down they could see the Cossacks riding down and killing some of their Jewish brethren. My great grandfather heard the rabbi say, "I wish I were God." He asked, "Do you want to be God so you can change the bad into the good?" "No, I wouldn't change anything. I want to be God so I can understand."

My entire life, I have shared this desire with the rabbi, this desire to understand.

When I was a young boy several of my friends died due to serious illness and one boy was hit by a car while bicycling to my house. I asked my father, "Why did God make a world where terrible things happen? Why didn't God make a world free of diseases, accidents and problems?" He said, "To learn lessons." I didn't like that answer and asked my rabbi, teacher, and others. They said things like, "That's life" or "To bring you closer to God." Some were honest enough to just say, "I don't know." When I told my mother what they said she offered, "Nature contains the wisdom you seek. Perhaps a walk in the woods would help you to find out why. Go and ask the old lady on the hill. She is one of the wisest people I know."

As I walked up the hill I saw a holly tree had fallen onto the path. As I tried to pull it aside the sharp leaves cut my hands. So I put on gloves and was able to move it and clear the path. A little farther along the path I heard a noise in the bushes and saw a duck caught in the plastic from a six pack. I went over and freed the duck and watched him fly off.

Farther up the hill I saw five boys lying in a tangled heap in the snow. I asked them if they were playing a game and warned them the cold weather could lead to frostbite if they didn't move. They said they were not playing but were so tangled they didn't know which part belonged to whom and were afraid they'd break something if they moved. I removed one of the boy's shoes, took a stick and jabbed it into his foot. He yelled, "Ow." I said, "That's your foot, now move it." I continued to jab until all the boys were separated.

As I reached the top of the hill I saw, in front of the old woman's cabin, a deer sprawled on the ice of a frozen pond. She kept slipping and sliding and couldn't stand up. I went out, calmed her and then helped her off the ice by holding her up and guiding her to the shore. I expected her to run away but instead of running away she followed me to the house. When I reached the porch I turned and the deer looked into my eyes.

I told the woman why I had come and she said, "I have been watching you walk up the hill and I think you have your answer."

"What answer?"

"Many things happened on your walk to teach you the lessons you needed to learn. One is that emotional and physical pain are necessary if we are to learn how to protect ourselves and our bodies. Think of why you put on gloves and how you helped those boys. Pain helps us to know and define ourselves and respond to our needs and the needs of our loved ones. You did what made sense. You helped those in front of you by doing what they needed when they needed it.

"The deer followed you to thank you, her eyes said it all. She was thanking you for being compassionate in her time of trouble. We are all here to continue God's work. If God had made a perfect world it would be a magic trick, not creation, with no meaning or place for us to learn and create. Creation is work. We are the ones who will have to create the world you are hoping for. We will still grieve when we experience losses, but we will also use that pain to help us know ourselves and respond to the needs of others. That is as the Creator intended it to be. God wants us to know that life is a series of beginnings not endings."

How do we turn our afflictions into blessings? How do we use them to help us complete ourselves and our work and understand the place for love, tolerance and kindness? Justice and mercy must both be a part of how we treat those who mistreat us because when you understand, you can forgive, and when you can forgive, you do not hate, and when you do not hate, you are capable of loving, and love is the most powerful weapon known to man. It is not an accident that we say, kill with kindness, love thine enemies, and torment with tenderness.

When we raise a generation of children with compassion, when parents make sure that their children know that they are loved, when teachers truly educate and not just inform, and when the clergy of every faith remind us that we are all children of God, we will have a planet inhabited by the human family, where our differences are used for recognition and not persecution, where we recognize that we are all the same color inside.

To paraphrase Rabbi Carlebach, let us hope that some day all the Cains will realize what they have done and will ask for forgiveness of all the Abels. In that moment we will all rise and become one family, accepting that we are here to love and be loved.

The "Artist" in Us All

Freddie Ravel

When I was somewhere around the age of four, I remember feeling the power of music tugging at my soul. Several years later, I started playing music and life has never been the same.

You know what the funny thing is? Music is really just a bunch of frequencies striking your eardrum, but when these frequencies vibrate in just the right way, something beyond words can happen. I still find myself in awe of the infinite combinations of melodies, harmonies and rhythms that make up what we call music. I describe it as a spirit whispering musical messages in my ears. It was through this "whispering" that I recognized my calling, my passion, for this muse.

Now for those of you in the arts, particularly musicians, you know that making a career in music is not for the squeamish. It requires constant practice and relentless dedication, and it is with this unbending devotion that I have spent the better part of my life traveling the world in little microcosms of bands and with other performing artists. It did not take long for me to feel and think of my life as a special "members only" type of club.

One night, as I was leaving a club after a performance, a man who was clearly homeless ran up to me and begged me to let him clean the windows of my car. Though my car was covered with the mist of the cold winter evening, I obliged. I began to study this man's face. He pulled out a soiled rag and a leaking spray bottle, and began the task. I have never seen anyone clean anything with so much dedication; those windows were scrubbed as if his life depended on it. His conviction, to clean so thoroughly, inspired me to give him a $20 bill. With a great sigh and a flood of tears he very graciously accepted.

I asked him his name.

"Timmy Young," he replied while fixing a gaze on me.

"What do you really do for a living?"

"Actually, I dance," he answered.

"What do you mean you dance?" His face brightened and in a proud posture he replied: "Well, my training was actually at the St. Louis Conservatory of Modern Dance and over the years I have appeared in all sorts of shows! I had a twist of fate when my mother passed away and I came to L.A. to be with my aunt. It turned out that her home was on the verge of slipping away from her and without a base I found myself here in the streets washing windows."

The story was told with such calmness that I knew it to be truth. I happened to be wearing a vest that had always been a "good luck" garment for me and I presented it to this kindred artist, this dancer. As tears filled his eyes, he gently reached for my hand and after a warm handshake followed by a beautiful double spin that would have made Baryshnikov proud, we bid each other farewell.

As I drove onto the freeway I felt myself beginning to cry and realized that the true gift of this encounter was really from Timmy to me.

You see, from that day on, I began to look at every human being in a new light. I now know that every person is filled with gifts, and regardless of outer appearances, we all have something very magical to share and express. There truly is an artist in us all.

AGAPE

Jimmi Ware

I am beautiful like a butterfly
Flittering here and there
Blessed with colors from many others
When I shed my cocoon

My dreads are carefree
That's alright by me
I am those beautiful colors
Of my fore-mothers
You know, that multi-racial facial
The one you cannot get from a salon
Nor from a jar of Ponds

It gives me great joy
To realize that brown eyes
Never made me blue
And blue eyes never made me green
With envy, it's not in me

My cousin sports a blonde curly afro
With pride, he loves the dark-berry beauty by his side
Is this a meeting of the United Nations?
Nah, just my family on vacation

We are simply family, beautiful like a rainbow
Radiant wherever we go, loving & kind
Understanding that the world needs more love
So we pour love and hope that it drenches you
Pass it on and on and on until "we" become "One"

ONE

Megan Katherine Dahle

One is a number but not only a number,
It is often forgotten as if it's in slumber,
So many look to higher figures,
And often forget of one's own signature,
One may not seem as much as far as money goes,
But one point won the game and so now one shows,

One vote refused Texas' entry into the Union,
One wrong turn leaves us in states of confusion,

One second sliced a new world record and won the gold,
One opening in the covers leaves your whole body cold,
One statement of truth that was never spoken,
Turns into a secret and an unused token,
One untrue rumor spread with cruelty,
One innocent victim foreseen as guilty,
One misunderstanding that was never made clear,

Hits one heart with a bloody spear,
One child who is hurt with words of hate,
Stands out in a crowd and is looked to as bait,
One bystander that stood there and saw it all,

Decides not to speak and just lets them fall,
One 'hello' or 'how are you' could have saved their day,
But one lived in fear of what the group would then say,
If only one person had the courage to stand up and be strong,
The one would have saved one person from
misery, evil and wrong,
One is a lot as far as I am concerned,
One could have saved many who anguished and yearned,

Whoever on earth thinks one is worth nothing,
Wasn't aware that one is truly something,
One changes and multiplies and causes results,
One gives us our victories and amplifies our faults,

If only we could just be the one in a world
that has withdrawn,
Then maybe we would be one in harmony
and all hatred would be gone.

Part II

Celebrating Diversity

~

This world is like a flower. Each nation is a petal. If one petal is infested, does it not affect all the other petals? Does not the disease destroy the life and beauty of the flower? Is it not the duty of each one of us to protect and preserve the beauty and fragrance of this one world flower from being destroyed? The world of ours is a big and wonderful flower with many petals. Only when this is understood and becomes deeply engrained within us, will there be any real peace and unity.

—Sri Mata Amritanandamayi Devi (Amma)

THE BLACK ROSE

Michele Wallace Campanelli

"Marlene, why aren't you talking to me anymore? I went to your house and you wouldn't answer the door. You won't walk with me to class either. What's going on?" Desperate to find out why my friend of two years was no longer speaking to me, I followed her into gym class.

"You'll be late for Driver's Ed," she snipped.

"What is going on? I thought you cared about me!"

"I did," Marlene turned and faced me. "Until you started hanging around Mike."

She slammed the gym door in my face. Not having the time to follow her, I hurried to the parking lot where my third period class was beginning. Four Driver's Ed cars were already weaving around the cones on the blocked-off parking lot.

Mr. Shultz, my teacher, glared at me. "Late again?" He groaned.

"Sorry, sir."

"Get to the back of the line," he said.

I hardly cared about placement. I was angry that Marlene didn't want to be friends anymore just because I had started dating Mike. He was such a sweetheart, opening doors, giving me roses and boxes of candy. A total gentleman, he hadn't even tried to kiss me yet. Perhaps he would tonight, on our third date.

Suddenly from the football field behind me, I heard my name being called. I turned and saw Marlene's brother, Ryan, hanging over the fence.

"Hey," he said.

I stepped from the back of the driver's line and walked several yards to the fence. "Hi, Ryan."

"My sister's mad at you," he removed his helmet. His head glistened in the sun.

"Yes, I know it's because of Mike. Why? Does she have a crush on him?"

"A crush?" he chuckled. "Don't think so. I'm willing to talk to you because I don't think you know what you're dealing with."

"What do you mean?" I asked.

Behind his uniform, Ryan pulled out a rose. It was like no other rose I had ever seen. I didn't even know roses came in that color. It was black, beautiful, and just opening its velvety petals.

"I started working at Gloria's flower shop down the street."

"I know." Marlene had mentioned it to me a few weeks ago. I remember thinking how unusual—a big macho guy selling flowers.

"Gloria's was the only place that would let me work around my football schedule. I drive the delivery truck," he said.

"Why black?" I asked, staring at the rose." Are you mad at me too?"

"No," he smiled. "Why do white people always think black means bad?"

"So it's a gift?" I asked.

"Yup."

I took the rose from him, carefully, so as to avoid catching my finger on a thorn. I had to admit, it was an amazing flower. Its dark petals shimmered with highlights of blue. Near the stem was a hint of purple. "Thank you. I love it!"

"Mike came in and bought you some roses yesterday." Ryan said. "Well, actually, he said, 'Get me a dozen roses, N———.' But I figured they were for you since you are dating him now."

I gasped, wondering if Mike actually used that word. "Maybe he meant it as a joke. Like you guys call each other that 'N' word."

Ryan smiled. "Why do you think he shaves his head?"

"Because he likes that wrestling star. Oh, what's his name? That Austin guy. He likes him. That's why he shaves his head. Is that what all this is about? You think Mike's a racist? Listen, he's not! Lots of guys shave their heads, that doesn't mean that they're into the KKK. I wouldn't hang out with someone who was like that. I'm not a racist; you know that. I wouldn't be best friends with Marlene if I was!" The moment I announced that, I painfully remembered Marlene no longer wanted to be friends with me.

"You know it's a funny thing about flowers," continued Ryan. "They come in all different colors and what they don't come in, people dye them. There are white, red, yellow, even blacks in demand now. But no matter the color, a rose still got thorns. Some people only see the thorns and not the flower, no matter how beautiful the bud is."

Confused, I studied his gift. "Ryan, if Mike were a racist I would know it."

"Here, comes Mr. Friendly now." Ryan stopped leaning over the fence and began staring over my shoulder.

Someone grabbed my arm and spun me around. "You're taking a flower from him?" Mike grabbed the top of the stem and pulled it from my hand. Thorns dug into my skin and ripped across my fingers. My blood spurted out as he threw the flower to the ground.

Ryan jumped the fence and looked at my hand. "You okay?"

"Stop talking to her!" Mike removed his shirt; then pushed Ryan against the fence.

I forgot about the pain in my hand. My attention was targeted on the words tattooed below Mike's neck: "W-H-I-T-E P-O-W-E-R."

Afraid for Ryan, I roared. "Let him go! He's my friend!"

"Friend?" Mike punched Ryan in the stomach. "Don't ever call one of these people your friend. They are the reason this country is falling apart. Affirmative action, welfare—don't you know you are part of the superior Aryan race! They ain't nothing but slaves bringing down the white man's world."

I could barely believe the words coming out of his mouth. Mike wasn't kind or thoughtful; he was a racist, a skin head, a white supremacist. He was a hater of Blacks, Asians, Hispanics, Jews, Gays and anyone not white and Protestant. Who knows—he might even loathe more groups. Why hadn't I seen this before?

Suddenly, I heard a chorus of voices chanting, "Fight! Fight! Fight!"

The entire line of students who had been waiting their turn to drive in the cars now circled us. The football players jumped the fence. Students divided into two separate groups: the blacks and the whites. Dozens took sides, glaring at each other, itching for a fight.

By now Mr. Shultz had pushed his way to the middle. "Get back to your classes! All of you! No trouble today."

No one was listening.

Mike suddenly turned to me. "Get out of here before war breaks out!" He yelled. "I'll see you later."

"No, you won't," I said. "I'm ashamed I ever dated you in the first place. Don't ever call me again."

Mike backed away from Ryan. "What? You're going to break up with me over this monkey?"

The African Americans in the crowd moved closer.

Ryan pushed them back. "Not over him! Not over this loser! He's not worth being cut from the team or even suspended! Come on, let's go!" Slowly, one by one, the football players followed Ryan back over the fence.

Now Mr. Shultz yelled along with the football coach, "Everyone get back to class! Hurry up."

The crowd dispersed. Racial war was somehow averted.

"Good-bye, Mike." I announced when he turned to me.

He put back on his shirt, tucking the shirttail back into his jeans. "That's fine with me, witch. If that's how you feel, you're not good enough for the Aryan nation."

"I think that's the nicest thing you've ever said to me."

"N—— lover!" He pivoted and stormed off.

With so much hate in his heart, I knew Mike wasn't for me. I also knew why Marlene was upset, and I completely understood that I owed her an apology.

Slowly, I bent over and picked up Ryan's black rose. It had lost a few petals but it was still remarkable. The ironic thing was Mike had also given me flowers before our last date: white rosebuds which never opened. Perhaps like their owner they just didn't know how to grow.

I Have Not Forgotten

Kim Huong Marker

Cumberland, Maryland, is a working middle-class neighborhood with split-level ranchers and two-story brick houses on manicured lawns. Flowerbeds, rock gardens, and a vast array of outdoor bric-a-brac adorn the front yards and porches of these homes.

On Bedford Street, a house is draped with four different versions of the American flag, and a patriotic plaque of a bald eagle hangs above the front entry. The flag that stands out—a black and white one that hangs at the end of the porch and simply states, "You are not forgotten."

The veterans, dead and missing, from the Vietnam War have not been forgotten in the minds of my parents. This war, which caused suffering, heartache, destruction, and death, consequently gave me a life, for it was during this conflict that my soldier-father met a young Vietnamese woman and fell in love. He married and brought her to the United States following the birth of their daughter and preceding the fall of Saigon. If time and history had occurred differently, I would be writing my story in Vietnamese, wondering about my American soldier-father. As fate would have it, though, I came to reside in the house on Bedford Street shrouded in American flags. I have not forgotten my fortune.

I grew up in a fusion of two ethnicities. We ate ginger rice with fried chicken and pho noodle soup, along with grilled cheese sandwiches. My weekly chores included dusting off my mother's Buddha and my father's bible, both sitting next to each other on the living room coffee table. All of my father's Christian and antique relics were intricately placed around the house with my mother's Asian artifacts.

My parents combined the disciplines of my father's Protestant work ethic and my mother's Asian filial piety as their models for child rearing, so that my brother and I would grow up to be honest, hard-working and loyal to our family. During my years of teenage angst, I displayed to my parents a learned sassiness never taught by them. My mother's stern hand of silence across my face helped me to remember disrespect was not accepted kindly in the house with the flags, a lesson I have yet to forget.

Despite my mother's efforts, the dominant American culture prevailed in our lives. By choosing to leave her native land, she chose to leave her native family. She adopted more of the American culture, which left her little time to model Vietnamese attributes for my brother and me. We never learned her language for she was too busy teaching herself English. She dressed us as average American children to shield us from the stabbing ridicule of youngsters who did not understand cultural diversity. She was careful with retelling old family tales and memories of her kin so as not to reopen a pain.

I remember watching my mother bundle care packages of American goods to send to Vietnam with the hope that her loved ones would receive them. In her tear-stained eyes, I could see she would never forget about or stop caring for her family, regardless of time or distance.

The messages in my father's eyes were not so clear. I yearned to know what those eyes had seen in those jungles where he found his true love. On asking him, he would bow his head and claim not to remember. When he did tell stories, he displayed a hypnotic, if not almost catatonic, stare. I learned to become sensitive to this defense mechanism of his. My father maintained ignorance, probably because he remembered too much.

I am not the greatest chef of either Vietnamese or American cuisine. I am not bilingual and do not celebrate every American holiday or participate in every Vietnamese custom. I cannot recount every fact or detail about the war. What I have inherited from my parents are the values of tolerance and independence. I was gifted with the ability to face uncertainty and loss with an inner strength, not only to survive, but to continue living. I was empowered to set goals and work hard toward achieving them. I was taught to love and respect myself. I have not forgotten these things my parents taught me, and I hope to always remember them.

I'm Not Black, I'm Brown

Beatrice M. Rembert

Red is a pretty color like cherries and strawberries, don't you think?

If strawberries are red then why is strawberry ice cream pink?

Orange is a pretty color that I like to see.

Pumpkins, oranges, and the fall leaves.

Well, we all know that the sun is yellow and the sky is blue.

The grass is green and grapes are too.

Grapes are green and purple, and that's a fact.

But did you know? I am white, and you are black!

I'm not black, that color is not me.

Have you taken a look at the color black lately?

It's the color of night without the moon and the stars.

It's the color of the roads that we drive our cars.

I know you can see that the color black is not the same as me!

I am brown, like peanut butter, cinnamon, or coffee with cream.

And guess what, you are not white, or am I seeing things?

The clouds and cotton is white and so are blank sheets.

Your skin is not white; your skin is peach,

When you really think about it, there is no black or white.

Instead there's all kinds of skin colors some dark, some light.

Different shades of browns, peaches, yellows, reds and pinks.

All of them are beautiful and all make me think…And say,

What difference does it make the color of my skin?

I have a name and I will share it with you my friend.

CRAYON

Sarah Kay Kessler

⌒

Crayons. Just their smell and the waxy feel as I pull them out of that bright yellow box are enough to remind me of my childhood....

In elementary school, I was the short, unusually tan girl in the front of the school bus who always had that dorky jacket, the four eyes, the affable crooked smile, and a weird medical patch over one eye that would later earn her the name "pirate girl." Ostracized early for things beyond my control, I quickly understood my first lesson about being different: I should be like a crayon because crayons of all colors learn to live together in the same box. Thinking and living this was sometimes harder than it sounded. I was young, and had trouble understanding why people singled me out.

I soon became involved in many activities that, for my age, were considered somewhat outside of the box. Starting in eighth grade, mentoring, tutoring, playing, and drawing dreams with elementary kids became an important part of my life.

One day, while scouring the classroom for the glittery, razzamatazz crayon that a little girl needed to finish her picture, I felt a little hand tap my shoulder and heard a small voice ask me, "Excuse me, are you Chinese?" Surprised that this little girl had the courage to ask, I replied, "No, I'm Korean," and gave her a reassuring smile to let her know it was all right to ask questions.

She turned to her friend who asked her what I had said. The words she said affected me more than any criticism, insult, or compliment I had ever received before.

She whispered back, "I think she said she's a crayon...."

ALMOST SISTERS

Elizabeth Blair

~

As a teenager in the early nineties I worked after school at a childcare center located in a suburb of Dallas. The center had children from many nationalities and cultural backgrounds. These children had grown close to each other because they had spent the last couple of years together. Often they resembled siblings, fighting, playing, singing, and dancing together.

One afternoon, my class and I had just finished the two o'clock snack. As we began cleaning up, one of the little girls, Mandy, took the initiative to get the hand broom while another girl, Trish, grabbed the dustpan. Together they worked as a team, sweeping the crushed goldfish crackers off the floor.

"Thank you girls for being such great helpers," I said. "You sure do work well together." "We're almost like sisters," Trish said. "Yep, almost like sisters," Mandy echoed. The girls giggled.

After our cleanup-time, the children went into the play center for "free play." I sat on a miniature orange chair and began cutting shapes out of construction paper for our afternoon art project. It wasn't long into playtime when Mandy and Trish walked up to me holding hands. Sitting in the small chair I was right at eye level from the girls. They both were grinning. I put down my scissors and looked at them.

"Hi, girls, are you having fun?"

"Oh, yes! But we have something very important to tell you," Mandy said.

"What is it?" I asked. They were so excited. I figured they were going to tell me they were going to spend the night at each other's house over the weekend.

Trish's eyes grew big. "Miss Beth, we just *learned* something!" she said proudly." I searched for a hint of their discovery.

"What did you learn, girls?"

"Well, me and Trish are different," Mandy said. The girls squeezed each other's hand.

I felt a smile creep over my face. The girls were the same age, same height, and both only children. But that's where the similarities ended. Trish was a beautiful little black girl with short dark hair, huge dark brown eyes and a perfectly white smile. Mandy was also beautiful. She had a fair complexion, long, curly, blond hair and big blue eyes. When she smiled she had dimples in both cheeks.

I nodded my head. "Yes, you are different, everyone is different. But tell me why you think you're different," I said. It had never occurred to me that they weren't aware of their differences. The subject of race had never been brought up in the entire three years I had been their preschool teacher.

The girls looked at each other and smiled. Mandy grabbed a strand of her hair and Trish grabbed one of her short braids.

"Don't you see?" Mandy asked, almost shocked at my ignorance. Holding the end of her ringlet Mandy said, "I have long blond hair and Trish has short brown hair." The girls began giggling again, celebrating their difference.

I smiled and said, "You're right, you do have different hair!"

Still holding hands, the girls turned around and began to walk back to the playhouse and I heard Trish say, "I want to be the big sister this time." Mandy giggled in return, "Okay, I'll be the little sister today."

The four-year-old girls didn't realize it, but they were exactly what sisters are supposed to be.

Far From Home

James Gerard Noel

Looking out the plane's window, I watched the white clouds mixing with the shades of gray beginning to invade the sky. I began to think of the life that lay before me in the United States. "What will my host family be like? Who are they? Will they like me?"

I knew how much I would miss my mother and older sister in England. Coming home on a Sunday evening and smelling the aroma of my mother's West Indian cuisine was going to be a thing of the past. And having intense arguments about anything and everything with my sister, then making up two hours later, was no longer going to be a part of my daily routine. I was just hours away from leaving that life for what seemed like forever.

I did know some information about my host family. I knew that the woman's name was Cindy and she was of Japanese descent. The man's name was David and he was Caucasian. They had two boys. There were some white people that married relatives in my family and I did have white friends in England, but I had never lived with anyone that was white. In addition, I did not know anyone who was Japanese, and I had this demented idea that every Asian person was an expert in the field of martial arts. I began to shake my head, trying to rid myself of all these thoughts, and it wasn't long before I managed to fall sound asleep.

When we finally landed and made our way through customs, I took a deep breath and confidently walked down the carpet into the heart of San Francisco's Airport. My eyes searched the crowds looking for my host family, and a small choir of people began to yell my name. They quickly made their way toward me and gave me a warm hug. Cindy was a very small lady, with smiling eyes and a motherly look to her. David was slightly taller than his wife and looked like he had a very creative and unique sense of humor. The two boys were quite small and hid their eyes underneath the beaks of their baseball caps, occasionally looking up and smiling.

That evening we made our way home to the town of Modesto, which is a couple hours from San Francisco. California was nothing like England; palm trees filled the sidewalks and the sun shone brightly and warmly. When we arrived at their home it was very well furnished and had an overall friendly aura to it. My bedroom was very spacious with a large window facing the street.

Initially, I was extremely bashful and only ate when food was offered to me. Weeks later I developed a good relationship with the refrigerator and all of the snack cupboards. I also learned more about my new host family. David owned his own carpentry business, enjoyed music and had an appetite for anything that had a raspberry and chocolate taste to it. Cindy took care of the business affairs, did not know martial arts and was a great cook. Whenever I got into any mischief, I felt as though I had a second mother. I would get a lecture from my mother in England and Cindy. Jordan was the youngest of the boys and he shared many of my interests, especially in sports. Garret was the elder boy and was an excellent student.

During high school, my "adopted family" showed me tremendous support by attending many of the sporting events that I participated in. After home football games, they would swarm around me, as if I were a professional. Cindy was my biggest fan and she wore my away jersey to all of my home games.

When I played basketball, members of the crowd would ask Dave if he had a relative playing on the court. He would reply, "My son," pointing me out. Surprise filled their faces, as they could not comprehend how a five-foot, small white male and Japanese female could have a child who was black, six feet seven inches, with a British accent.

Growing up, I always wanted to be the "eldest" in my household, and when I came to California I evolved into one. Jordan and Garrett are like my younger brothers. I teach them the fundamentals of baseball and other things I have learned about the game. We argue like typical American siblings.

Since my arrival, I graduated from high school and am now a student-athlete at Modesto Junior College in California. During that plane journey into San Francisco I did not know what to expect. However, I now realize how blessed I am. I have learned to welcome our diversity and to embrace my host family's culture along with mine. I would not want it any other way.

KUN IMMO

Margaret Cho

⸻

Kun Immo was not her name, but it was what we called her. Kun in Korean means "big" and Immo is "Aunt;" She was my mother's oldest sister, and in Korea, as it is in the army, you are known more for your rank, where you stand in the lineup, than who you actually are.

Kun Immo fit her well anyway, because she was a big aunt, tall like a tree and with a booming, raspy voice and a giant's laugh, so different from the delicate flowery women in the rest of my family. She would come to our house in San Francisco, when my brother and I were small, and scoop us up in her big, soft hands and love us with a hoarse laugh and a tender ferocity. I was never afraid of her, or tentative, as I felt with so many of my relatives. There was an anything goes, Auntie Mame quality—a feeling like you could get away with anything in her presence; she was that easy. She was a "Take two, they're small" and "If you don't have anything nice to say, sit next to me" kind of lady, and I am her direct descendant. Her daughter was a small version of her, a modern artist, but not as easy to be with. She had a tightness around her, a brittle heart encased in her thin frame. She lived in a high-rise in Seoul, with a beautiful and bratty baby boy and sculptures of human hands grabbing all over the place.

Kun Immo dispensed the kind of love that whenever you saw her, even if it was only five minutes before, she would act like she hadn't seen you in a million years. She could not contain herself or her affection. She was too big, too bursting with everything good. I remember surprising her in the bathroom, huge in her bathrobe, face covered in cold cream, looking like a man in drag. She smiled and waved even though I was only three feet away and had just seen her at breakfast. Kun Immo pulled me into my bedroom, which was where she was sleeping, and opened up her giant's suitcase. It smelled of mothballs and camphor, the elemental scent of my homeland, and out came crumpled wads of tissue paper containing miniscule treasures: rings in tiny satin bags, gold that she would bite and bend to prove it was real. She'd put it on my finger and laugh that thundering laugh and shake the walls. She couldn't stop pulling things out of her case.

She'd give me gifts meant for others and make excuses for herself—blaming her forgetfulness, promising an even more costly trinket next time, with a wink at me from across the room, as I wore her glittery secrets on my fingers. Such was the force of her love. She was unstoppable, a mighty river, and when we were kids we would ride her white water in jade and gold. I knew her husband was rich, and her house in Korea had an imposing concrete wall around it, a driver day and night, and giant beetles like flat centipedes that moved faster than light that invaded the bath.

Of course, I never went to see her when she was dying. And I knew it was serious because my mother, at some point, had stopped asking me. It was always in the back of my mind, her illness, my selfish fear of seeing her diminished. I think I made an attempt very near the end, a suggestion to my mother that I might join her on one of her many trips to the hospital. Her reply was a kind but firm, "No, it better not. Because she cannot see or know you anyway. It is okay, but she cannot see you. You just may be upset. You cannot understand this kind of thing. Too young to understand. You don't want to see her. She too thin." It is so ironic, that the thinness I have longed for my entire life, comes for some of us only in death.

I guess I was relieved. So we left it there. My selfishness and my youth saved me from having to look at death in the form of my favorite aunt, and I could keep her memory, as a large and laughing beautiful woman, unable to stop herself from giving me gifts.

Kun Immo's cancer had spread throughout her entire body; the disease, as unstoppable as her love. There was nothing else for the accomplished American oncologists, the best the big money could buy, to do. She was put on a plane to Seoul, so that she might die in her big house, surrounded by her great walls and her many children and grandchildren and the driver and the beetles.

She didn't make it. She died somewhere over Seattle. The plane had to make an emergency landing. Passengers were unwilling to share the plane with this dead woman, even though this dead woman had once been alive, had once had cold cream all over her face and had once been so loved by a little girl. I don't know why the stewardesses didn't just put a blanket over her, a sleeping mask, maybe some Bose headphones—pretended that she was asleep while listening to Celine Dion. The plane landed, and my Kun Immo was taken to the morgue.

My mother had to drive all the way to Seattle, to the coroner's office, to identify the body. Kun Immo had been dead for some time. It only takes a few minutes for rigor mortis to set in, so imagine what many hours might do. My mother didn't care, and cried and hugged her sister and kissed her and could not, would not, let her go, all the while apologizing to her for having to die up there, all alone, at 35,000 feet, in the middle of a Korean Air flight, caught between here and home, in the nowhere of air and sky.

It makes me sick to think of my mommy at the morgue, surrounded by the cold, blue staff, the people who have probably seen every conceivable kind of pain, standing around waiting for this crazy Korean woman to finish so they could wrap up the body and ship it out. I wish they could have known the woman that was on the slab. That she was once a giantess, unstoppable and huge, with a heart bursting with love and presents. I wish that everyone could have a Kun Immo, staying in their bedroom, hugging their children hard, unapologetically loving them for all time.

CHECK THE CORRECT ETHNIC BOX

LaVonne Schoneman

Do not paint me with your paintbrush
Coloring me in blackest hue
I am quite unique and different
From the others facing you
My skin is dark—my hair is too
My eyes are rather greenish-hue
They slant a little
And that is why
To check this box
Is to deny
My Asian mother
My grandma too
Who brought from Germany
Eyes of blue
An ancestor's blood
From Africa
Flowed
Through Tahiti where
It finally
Showed
As a mix in the veins

Of my father who
Expressed
Genetically
It's true
This ethnic
Unique
Person you
See standing here
Pen poised
Just so
Hovering
Above
The defining square
Of who I am
This isn't fair
To check each racial box
Would be
Redundant, hapless
Foolery
Don't put me in
Some category
To suit your needs
Be prejudice-free
Then keep in mind
This simile
Tolerance
Unlatches locks
On
The misbegotten
Bigotry box.

PART III

ONE IN SPIRIT

If we have listening ears, God speaks to us in our own language, whatever that language be.

—Mahatma Gandhi

Escuchar, the Wind

Shinan Naom Barclay

In the wildness of the north wind, I walked the bay, where white caps tumbled across the inlet's surface. Desperate for solace, I was intent on feeling swept clean by the blustery ocean breeze. I am a caregiver for three patients—cervical cancer, quadruple bypass, broken hip. And now, in the past two weeks, four of my own loved ones have been diagnosed—tendinitis, diabetes, breast cancer, and a brain tumor. I needed time with nature and to be alone.

So I walked two miles to this shoreline park, where sand and surf vie for the boundary of the southern Oregon coast. Zipping up my windbreaker, I watched gulls ride the updraft. Then I climbed the jetty stones, eased my way down to the sand, and there slipped off my shoes and socks and hid them between two boulders.

Climbing a knoll of beach grass, I walked to the familiar log where I always stop. That's when I saw him. A dark stranger. Neither fisherman nor crabber. By his demeanor, I knew this was not a native Californian. He appeared to be Hispanic. I had many Hispanic friends from school, our neighborhood and church. "Sing *'El Rancho Grande,' por favor*," I'd request of the mariachis playing guitars in our neighborhood park. Parental warnings, "Don't talk to strangers," never worked with me. From the time I could walk, I was one of those children who never saw a stranger. I ran to meet anyone different from me.

But now I am a mature woman, alone on a long stretch of deserted beach. I know better than to put myself in risky situations. I decided to continue walking, to keep my distance from the dark stranger, and to stay within sight of some people sitting in a car in the parking lot. I walked the higher trail, along the uppermost embankment of beach grass; he walked the lower trail—near crashing waters. The cuffs and shirttails of his white shirt flapped in the wind. I noticed his trim black hair, short except for a duck curl at the back of his neck. His head lowered, he read a small book; pages turned as he walked down the beach. I wondered what he was reading—bible verse, a novel, a comic book?

In our zigzag walks along the sea, the man and I passed each other twice. Then he stopped and smiled, revealing brilliant white teeth. "*Hola.*" He looked clean-cut and freshly shaven with ironed khaki trousers, brown loafers and the small book rolled up in his hand. "*Hola,*" I responded with a guarded smile. No "uh-oh" feeling in my gut.

"*Mucho frío.*" He rubbed his upper arms. The temperature had dropped quickly with the setting sun. Colors danced orange and purple along the glistening shoreline. The cloud bank along the horizon rolled inland. Through my windbreaker, I felt the chill. Cold is right, I thought, and this guy was wearing only a thin shirt.

"*Dondé está su…?*" Where is your…? I don't know the word for "jacket." I shake the vinyl collar of my windbreaker.

"*No tengo chaqueta.*" He shook his head and imitated a shiver. "*¿Habla usted Español?*"

"*Poquito.*" I pinched my index finger and thumb together, leaving a half-inch space. "*¿Habla usted Inglés?*"

"*No, no Inglés.*" He shook his head and shrugged.

"*¿No Inglés, porqué? Es no bueno.*" If he lives here, I wondered, why wouldn't he take advantage of an ESL (English as a second language) class? How could a person live in a country and not learn bits of the language? Perhaps he recently arrived or is just visiting. Then he answered my questions without my asking.

"*Yo vivo en las montañas de Mexico. Pero aquí, trabajo demasiado.*" He lives in the mountains of Mexico. But here he works a lot.

He leaned forward, bowed his back slightly, swayed his torso side to side and hummed "rrrrrrrrrrrrrrrrrrr." A weed eater! I knew that stance from times when I've whacked down laurel and salal.

"*Todo.*" He looked at the distant brush, quickly moving the flat of his hand sideways, indicating he has cut everything.

"*Mañana es Domingo. No trabajamos, y esta noche quiero encontrar el mar.*" Tomorrow is Sunday. No work. And tonight I want to encounter the sea.

I repeated the words in my mind, *quiero encontrar el mar*. I want to encounter the sea. I loved the rhythm and romance of the language. Although it has been years since I studied Spanish, I am pleased that I understand him.

"*¿Dondé está su esposo?*"

"*No esposo, no niños, solamente yo y Dios.*" No husband, no children, only me and God. I touched my heart and raised my hand to the sky.

"*¿Dios?*" He stared at me.

"*Sí.*" I'm a gringo trying to get my point across without much Spanish. "*Dios es mi favorito; es mi dulce de corazon .*" God is my favorite. God is my sweetheart; I'd never thought of my relationship with the Great Creator quite that way. But now hearing "God is my sweetness of heart," I like the feel and the sound. How do I explain to a stranger that I'm a loner? I prefer prayer to parties, solitude to socializing, and meditation to movies.

The salt sea breeze, cold and fresh on my face dissolved the stress and responsibilities of the past weeks. I had been washed by the wind; I felt clear, clean and free; felt energized. I loved that wind.

"Wind! *Cómo se dice...*" How do you say... I held my arms out and twirled around imitating the "wsshh." sound I heard. "Wind." I stepped forward and looked directly at him.

He stared at me. "*El viento.*" The wind.

We are strangers, a man and a woman alone on a deserted beach, now looking deeply into each other's eyes, not for romance or a flirtation, but to understand each other.

"*El viento es magnífico.*" The wind is magnificent. My mind flips through the photo album of memories: along the blustery Atlantic Ocean, my grandfather clutching my tiny two-year-old hand, the delicious salt sea air blowing in my face and up my nose. Wind gusting the sails of the schooner my sister Mary Lou and I, as Mariner Scouts, sail up the inland passage of British Columbia. Choosing motorcycles over cars for my main mode of transportation, as an adult, so I could be part of the wind.

Back on the beach, in a pantomime of gestures my closed hand reached my mouth, fingers exploding open, palm flat reaching up, skyward. "*La voz de Diós está en el viento.*" The voice of God is in the wind.

"*¿La voz de Diós está en el viento?*" He looked up as if searching the sky. "*¿Cómo y dondé?*" How and where? He asked as he wrinkled his eyebrows and looked at me intently with clear, dark eyes.

How and where? I groped for simple language, searching my memory for Spanish words. "*En el silencio*." In the silence and meditation. "*Y meditación*." With a slight shift of spelling and pronunciation, many English words translate into Spanish; I'm not sure if meditation is one, but I chance it.

"*¿Silencio y meditación en la iglesia, también?*" Silence and meditation in church, also?

"*Sí. Es verdad*." It's true. I tell him, But then he asks a more difficult question.

"*La voz de Diós está in la Biblia. Es verdad. ¿No?*" The voice of God is in the Bible. That's true, isn't it?

How do I answer a theological question in gringo Spanish? "*Para mi, ni iglesia, ni Biblia*." For me neither church nor Bible. I grasp for words to explain my belief, background, and present theological stance. "*Pero, mi madre es Católico, mi padre es Católico*." But my mother is Catholic, my father is Catholic. "*Por muchos años mi escuela es Católica*." For many years my school is Catholic. Words from my high school vocabulary list pop off the page in the Spanish text, as if I were back in Catholic school sitting at my laminated wood desk. Then I tell this stranger, "*La atmósfera poderosa son espíritus*." The powerful atmospheres are sacred spirits. Oh, the nuns would have a heart attack at my interpretations of both Spanish and religion. The Inuits and Hopi, however, taught me about Thunderbeings and the Spirit Keepers of wind, rain, and sky. I reached for the lobes of my ears and wiggled them back and forth. "*Orejas aquí*." Ears here. But how do you say what happens within the ears? I stick my index fingers into my ears asking, "*Como se dice*. How do you say 'hear'?"

"*Oír*." He looked at me quizzically.

I wondered if he thought I was *loco*. Then his dark eyes moisten, he nodded and faintly smiled. I knew he understood. It isn't just empty hearing. It's really listening, listening with the heart. I cupped my right hand on one ear and put the other over my heart. "*Orejas de corazón*." Ears of the heart.

"*Muy bonita*." He nodded, and then cupped his right hand behind his right earlobe while placing his left hand over his heart. "Escuchar." Leaning toward the waves, he closed his eyes and for a moment was silent. Then he looked at me intently. "*Yo escucho a las olas*." I listen to the waves. He reached up toward the circling gulls; he bent his body toward leaves rustling on nearby willows, then slowly placed the palms of his hands over his heart, closed his eyes, and whispered, "*Escuchar*."

That's it. I remembered old Sister Irma Aloysius saying, "I don't want you to just *oír*, hear … I want you to *escuchar*, listen," and she would prayerfully place the palms of her hands over her heart and open them toward the class.

"*Yo escucho al viento*," I shouted. I listen to the wind.

"*Muy hermosa*." He smiled.

"*Sí, es muy hermosa. Gracias*." Yes, it is very beautiful. Thank you. I wanted to tell him that he had helped me understand. But I didn't have the words to explain so I told him what many indigenous people believe. "*Escucho la voz del espíritu grande en el viento*." I hear the voice of the Great Spirit in the wind. "*Muy bella*." He smiled, nodding his head.

"*Muchas gracias*." I wanted to hug him and say thank you— this stranger who has helped me understand what I love about the wind. We walked toward the parking lot. "*Me llamo es Shinan*." My name is Shinan. I stood up and reached out to shake his hand. As he took my hand, placing the rolled comic book in his left hand, I noticed the title, *Diccionario Primero de Español y Inglés*. First Dictionary of Spanish and English.

"*Me llamo Jórge. Jórge Robles.*" Tears stung my eyes as I felt his warm hand in mine.

"*Adiós*," I called out as I walked up the street.

"*Buena suerte*," he shouted ambling down the road. Good luck.

Walking home I reflected on the chance meeting with that gentle man, far from home, who came to encounter the sea. In telling him about my love for the wind, I explained it to myself. What a gift he gave me, that stranger with no *Inglés* and no jacket for warmth, that stranger who also walked along the edge, alone. He gave me *escuchar*, and I gave him the wind.

THE COLOR OF LOVE

Cheryl Costello-Forshey

A mother and her small young boy were walking through the
park
Stars were sprinkled in the sky, shining through the dark
The night was warm and peaceful, a breeze whisking through
the air
Blinded eyes plagued her son; a world she felt that she must
share
To understand the darkness, that besieged his life each day
And to pretend that night was morning, to her seemed the
perfect way
So together they journeyed forward, walking past the trees
Hearing the sound of the wind, rustling through the leaves
Talking at once and laughing, their hands together entwined
as one
Imagining that the surrounding dark sky, was filled with the
brightness of sun
Together they swung on the swing set, running through the
darkness at play
Him never seeing the difference that separated both night and
day

Living their lives in the moment, their bond growing increasingly strong

Make-believing, pretending, a world where nothing was wrong

But somewhere out of that darkness, a group of boisterous young men

Decided to take upon themselves, a chance to make peacefulness end

For they circled around that mother and son, laughing and calling them names

Epithets of the words black and white, their message to the mother quite plain

She desperately fought back her teardrops, as she pulled her son by the hand

Knowing too well the danger, of speaking out, taking a stand

Relief washed over her slowly, as she watched those boys turn away

For they had done what they'd longed to, they'd said all they needed to say

Silence followed the journey, as that mother and son walked alone

Their footsteps quick and eager, as they made their way back to home

At last they arrived at their doorstep, when the little boy finally asked

The question the mother now realized, she would have to answer at last

"Mommy I don't understand it, please tell me what I can't see

Mommy what color am I, are you the same color as me?"

What should she tell her child, about the difference in their color of skin

How could she explain biracial, where would she even begin

Her heart felt like a boulder, heavy and weighing down strong

The innocence of her son taken away, to lie to him now would be wrong

Her words came slowly at first, but from somewhere deep down inside

She spoke to her son the truth, her face blazing with pride

"My darling," she answered so softly, "you are a gift from the good Lord above

And the color of you is the same as me, we're both the color of love"

Instead of her knowing his darkness, a child was forced to see light

And where once he never saw colors, he now saw black and white

In a world where nothing is perfect, a little boy was made to feel shame

Not knowing the color biracial, but knowing that words can cause pain

But somehow he seemed to accept it; he was a gift from the good Lord above

And the only color that mattered to him was the color of love

THE TRUTH ABOUT ISLAM

Muhammad Ali

I first became interested in Islam in the early 1960s, during the movement led here in the United States by the Honorable Elijah Muhammad. At the time, I believed that what I was hearing in Elijah's mosques was the real Islam because it made sense to me as a young black man living in a segregated, racially explosive country. Elijah preached that all white people were devils. Because Elijah's followers were black converts, the white press named Elijah's group the Black Muslims. It was never a name that Elijah himself assigned to his followers.

Even though Elijah taught us to hate white people, I never really practiced it. I always had lots of different people around me, people of different races, creeds, and cultures.

I think my eyes began to open to the truth of real Islam when Malcolm X made his journey to Mecca. Malcolm was older than me, and in many ways I looked up to him like an older brother or mentor. Every devout Muslim is supposed to make a trip to Mecca at least once in his or her lifetime. During his pilgrimage to Mecca, Malcolm realized that there were Muslims of all colors from many different countries. When Malcolm went, it was a real turning point in his beliefs. He came back a different man. He stopped preaching black separatism and started talking about a more inclusive religion—the true Islam as it was practiced in Muslim countries around the world and prescribed in the

Qur'an. I made my own pilgrimage to Mecca, during Hajj, which is the annual pilgrimage when thousands of Muslims from all of the world make the journey, and I saw this for myself.

I was amazed to see how many different types of people were all part of Islam. I met Pakistanis, Indians, and Africans, but of course I considered them all to be people of color. I was surprised to meet Chinese, Malaysian, and Filipino Muslims, but really they were people of color as well. Then I met Muslims from Turkey, Russia, and Albania. These were white people, some with blue eyes and blond hair. I was just shocked! It was so different from what I had been taught. How could I call these white people devils if they were a part of our own?

Then I started to realize that there were lots of Americans and British who had converted to Islam as well, people like the singer Cat Stevens, who were white too.

I always knew, I guess, that you couldn't just divide people up that way. Maybe I just needed some visible evidence that proved the "White Devil" philosophy untrue. Even though I have changed my views on most of what Elijah taught, some of his philosophy I still hold to be true. For example, black people should be self-sufficient and shouldn't look for handouts or depend on others for opportunities. But I no longer believe his message of separation is true. That was never a tenet of Islam. In fact, Islam preaches just the opposite.

Unfortunately, these days, a lot of people associate Islam with violence, and I am always surprised by that. Islam means "peace." Our greeting—*Assalaam Alaikum*—means "Peace be unto you." Islam, as I understand it, means total submission to God. You cannot be violent when you have submitted your will to God. The entire religion of Islam is based upon the concept of peace.

I think Islam is probably the most misunderstood religion. Maybe because it is Eastern, it seems foreign to most Westerners.

Perhaps Hollywood's version of the Crusades has contributed to this fierce image of Islam. Muslims were portrayed as bloodthirsty marauders atop large dark steeds, wielding long swords and cutting wide paths of destruction across parts of Europe.

Our history classes don't do enought to correct this impression. The amazing contributions Muslims have made to the advancement of civilization are not given enought attention. Mathematics, science, medicine, architecture, and literature have all been advanced through Islamic influence. We use Arabic numerals every day. The oldest university in the world is Al-Azhar in Egypt. It was conceived, built, and maintained even to this day by Muslims.

Of course, people can destroy and manipulate and misuse anything. We as humans tend to do that. Some people have used Islam for their purposes, and turned it into something that it is not. But that doesn't make Islam itself a violent religion, any more than the Christian Crusades against the Muslims make Christianity a violent religion.

I learned about peace through Islam, which is why I did not go to Vietnam. Islam is what helped center me. It helped give me the courage not to go and to stand up for my convictions.

The Army really tried hard to get me to go. They said, "If you go to Vietnam, you won't have to fight or carry a gun, you could just do exhibition bouts like Joe Louis did." But I didn't care. In my mind if I had gone I would still have been aiding and abetting the killing of innocent people—people who'd never done anything to me. I don't mind fighting in self-defense, but these people never attacked my family, my country, or me. We went over there attacking them, they didn't come after us! I thought, "There are people right here in America who don't respect me or my people and who would lynch my relatives if they could. Why should I be fighting over in Vietnam? I should be fighting over here!"

If there is something that God would want me to do, I don't care who says what, who gives what, who begs what; I don't care how much money they offer me: I am still going to do what God wants me to do and what I know is right in my heart. And that is what Islam has taught me. It has given me the courage, the centering, and the inner peace to be able to live that way.

I was once in New York City, listening to the radio. There was a human-interest story on the radio about an old folks' home that was going to be closed down because they did not have enough money to keep it open. I thought, "Where are these old people going to go?" This happened to be a Jewish home, but the residents were human beings, created and put here by God, and they were suffering. They had no one to take care of them; they were old, and they couldn't work or provide for themselves. So I called up the radio station and asked them how I could give the home $100,000 to keep it open.

They didn't believe me at first. They thought it was a prank, and that I was someone who was just pretending to be Muhammad Ali. I think because people knew I was a follower of Elijah Muhammad and a so-called "Black Muslim," they were surprised that I would give so much money to people who weren't Muslims and who weren't even Black.

I believe that we all belong to the human race, and it doesn't really matter what other race we want to call ourselves, because God made us part of the human race first. Maybe God made all of our other differences so that we could explore them and enrich our lives by learning about each other's culture and heritage.

There is a saying I always believe in that I think sums up a lot of what is true about religions, people, and cultures: "Rivers, lakes, ponds, and streams all have different names, but they all contain water." Just like all religions have different names—but they all contain truth.

Peace on Earth

Laura Stamps

Sometimes I am certain
the peace I feel, floating among
the silver leaves of early evening,
can surely travel from my fingertips
halfway across the blue mouth
of the sea to a country foreign
and fettered with men
squabbling among themselves
over politics or land or power,
until one suddenly notices
the apricot stain of this setting sun
and the silver-leafed trees,
his burden easing, and he turns
to another and says:
May we drop these stones,
cold and light-dazed, and find
a way to live in peace.

A Walk in the Clouds

Steven Manchester

I walked amongst the clouds today
and then I took a seat,
to try to understand the world
that spun beneath my feet.
It was the grandest picture
my eyes had ever seen.
I couldn't make out colors—
except for blue and green.
And yet, I could see people;
a whole race on the run.
To tell the truth, from where I sat,
they clearly moved as one.
With fear, they searched for answers
they thought were on the ground.
And though they spoke in different tongues,
they made the sweetest sound.
They had the wrong perspective,
with no way they could know:
There are no individuals,
but just parts of a whole.
And so I made a wish for them,
that someday they would see:
Only when they really love

is when they're really free.
I'll dance amongst the stars tonight,
while others search in vain.
For just above their point of view,
there's no such thing as pain.

PATHS TO THE CREATOR

Sharon Redhawk Love, Ph.D

On the reservation each week, different churches would come to do outreach to the Indians. One week, Baptists would come on Wednesday evening and have their ice cream social, returning on Sunday to offer church services and to reach the souls of the heathens. The next week, Methodists would come, have a dance during the week, and also return for services. The following week, a similar routine: Catholics would arrive with a dinner, then return on the weekend for services. And so it went week after week, group after group.

During this time, a young man goes to his grandfather in confusion.

"Grandfather, you have lived a long life. In my few years on this earth I have come to know your wisdom. Now Grandfather, I come to you for guidance. Each week they come to tell us the right way to live. Baptists tell us their way is the only way to the Creator, Methodists tell us their way is the way to the Creator. Then, Catholics come and say the same. Between these visits I go with Uncle to the Peyote circles and with Father to the sweat lodges. Grandfather, in your wisdom can you tell me which is the path to the Creator?"

The youth's grandfather smiles and says, "The answer you seek is in the tepee." He sends the grandson to investigate the tepee sitting in the grasses.

Grandson walks into the tepee and looks up, seeing the large circle above him, the flags flying in four colors above the outside of the tepee, and the sky of the Creator. He sees no answer. He then walks around the inside of the tepee, looking at the many poles it takes to hold up the tepee. He sees thick poles and thin poles. He sees straight poles and poles with imperfections, all leading to the circle at the top of the tepee. He continues examining the skin of the tepee, the many stitches it holds, the way it sits upon the earth, but he sees no answer.

Grandson then begins to walk the outside, round he goes. He looks at the effigies painted on the outside, the colors, the circle it forms. He looks at the stakes, which hold it firm, and he looks at the top, the smoke hole with flags in the wind. Impatiently, he returns to his grandfather, "Grandfather, I have looked in and around the tepee, I have seen nothing and I have found no answer." Grandfather smiles and encourages the grandson to return to the tepee once again, assuring him the answer is in there.

Again Grandson returns to the tepee, this time he walks around right to left, left to right, "Does Grandfather think I am stupid? There are no answers here." The grandson leaves filled with anger and disgust.

The next morning, feeling as though he may have acted in haste, Grandson returns to the tepee to look once more. He begins to speak, "Grandfather is playing coyote jokes on me." Grandson walks within the tepee, counts the poles, the stakes, the flags. He spends the entire day with the tepee. Grandson has made three visits but no answer is found.

In the morning Grandson returns to his grandfather still angry, "Grandfather, there are no answers in the tepee; you are sending me on a chase." Grandfather, smiles and tells his grandson he is not misleading him. Grandfather shares that in his youth he went to the tepee and it took many days to find the answer. He directs his grandson to return a fourth time to the tepee and sit within it, be with the tepee, listen carefully and walk about the tepee with a quiet heart, only then will he find the answer. Grandson agrees to make one more attempt.

The next day Grandson returns. "Grandfather, I stayed the entire day with the tepee, and I spent the entire night. I did everything you told me to do Grandfather and still I found no answer. Please help me Grandfather." Grandfather smiles and gives his grandson food and water and offers him his blanket to sit for a while. The Grandson is tired, both physically and in spirit. He is no longer angry and no longer sure he can find the answer to which was the right path to the Creator. He is frightened. Gently Grandfather sits beside the youth, and begins to share with him the wisdom of the tepee.

"Grandson, as you walked toward the tepee, what did you notice?"

"I saw the shape Grandfather, it seemed to point toward the Creator and I had hope."

"Grandson, what did you see when you walked inside the tepee?"

"Grandfather, I looked toward the Creator and saw the colors of all who walk this earth speaking prayers in the spirit wind to the Creator in the clouds above."

Grandfather then asks, "Grandson, what did you notice within the tepee as support."

Grandson thinks and says, "Do you mean the poles?"

Grandfather tells Grandson, "The poles support the tepee, but no one pole can do it alone. It takes all of the poles to do the job. Each week a different group comes to our land, and each week these groups tell you theirs is the only path to the Creator.

Grandson, the groups are like the poles of the tepee. All of them are needed, some are more perfectly suited to others, but they all point toward the Creator. You, my grandson must find your pole, and follow it to the Creator. It does not matter which pole you choose, but that you choose a pole to follow. You may change poles in your life, you may follow the sweat lodge pole for a time; then switch to one of the other poles, but never lose sight of the circle above you, the Creator and your path toward the Creator. When you are tired, the tepee will give you shelter. It will keep you within its sacred protection, but you must be willing to come and sit and listen to your spirit. You must be willing to sit in the spirit wind and send prayers of all colors to the Creator."

Grandson smiles, and hugs his grandfather. He begins to understand the answer in the tepee. Many years would pass before he understood the full answer, but Grandson had begun the journey.

The answer: *Mitakuye oyasin*—a Lakota Sioux expression that translates as "we are all connected."

Symphony of Prayer

Rabbi Jack Reimer

Shmuel Avidar grew up in the Old City of Yerushalayim. But from 1948 to 1967, while the Old City was in the hands of the Arabs, he could not go there. A barbed wire cut through the middle of the city, and he could only look at it from afar.

Then in 1967, Yerushalayim was reunited once again. Shmuel Avidar ran to the city to see the streets, the neighborhood, and the house where he lived as a child. He went to the door and asked the Arabs who lived there if he could come in and look around, and they allowed him to do so.

After he had gone through the house he wandered onto the balcony, the same balcony where he, as a child who could not sleep, would go out and watch for the sun to rise.

He remembered hearing the sound of his Zeidi and the other pious Jews praying through the night at the Kotel. Then he would hear the sound of the Muzzein calling the faithful to pray in the mosque, just above the Kotel. At the same time, he used to hear the sound of the church bells, summoning the Christians to come to pray. He used to wonder: which of these prayers: those of the Jews, those of the Muslims, or those of the Christians, did God live to hear the most?

One day he asked his Zeidi that question. His Zeidi told him that to us these sounds, the Jews reciting Tikkun Hattsot, the Muslims being called to prayer by the Muzzein, and the church bells summoning the Christians, come as a cacophony of noise. But to God, these sounds blend and form a symphony.

OLD TIME RELIGION

Deborah C. Thomas

In India, there are many beautiful Hindu temples. I had read about one such temple in the Rajasthan region. One evening, prior to sunset I went there alone.

I removed my shoes outside of the temple entrance while taking mental notes of the beggars. Several women sat in a circle making garlands of flowers. Everyone was watching me and I was watching everyone. One woman, in particular, seemed to be reading my thoughts. She had hands just like my mother's hands. Her jewelry and manner of dress indicated that she was not poor yet she sat with the poor. Something in her wise dark eyes conveyed to me that all I left behind would be safe. She would be the guardian. And so, I left all of my valuables, tucked inside my satchel, along with shoes in her keeping.

Once inside of the temple, my bare feet felt at home on the cool stone floors. I paused to admire a statue of Nandi the bull. His golden girdle blending with the softness of candle light stirred me as did the chanting of the devotees. There was this feeling of déjà vu. My soul reminded me "you have been here before." I sat with the devotees, most of whom were women. Their chanting was celestial. They were chanting the name of God, "Jai Ram," in four-part harmony, in call and response form. Seeing and hearing them reminded me of my grandmother and the mothers in the sanctified church. The rhythm of the small hand cymbals became for me the tambourines and foot stompings of my church back home. How many times, as a child, had I been a witness to those elderly women dressed in white, calling on Jesus, while rocking in time to their prayers. I was waiting for someone to really get happy and shout because as the old folks used to say: "The Spirit was moving."

And then I heard a shriek. When I opened my eyes I saw them. Rats. They were everywhere, running and scampering all over the temple. The devotees didn't seem to mind. The chanting never ceased. I wondered who screamed. And then I saw a middle aged European woman with a Nikon camera dangling from her neck running toward the exit, saying "This is disgraceful." One of the temple attendants was saying something to her in response. When the rats gathered around the attendant's feet I found myself examining my own feet. "Shiva" I said to myself, "You are being a trickster again." Darkness tipped into the temple. The chanting dwindled to a distant hum. Prayer meeting was over.

The devotees began to leave. I followed them outside where my shoes and satchel were waiting, next to their guardian. The woman's eyes had kept their promise. When I approached her, she placed a garland of marigolds around my neck. "Om Shanti" I whispered, with clasped hands in front of my heart center. When I placed a small payment in her hands, hands that looked so much like my mother's, she gave it to the crippled woman beside her.

I walked away from the women's circle into the crowd of vendors selling incense, kabobs, postcards, and mala beads. I thought for a moment about the rats. Surrounded by a quartet of beggars I could hear that woman shouting "This is disgraceful!"

Yet, I did not feel that way. Instead, smiled. Shiva's laughter echoed in the night. The Spirit was moving.

20/20 SOUL VISION

Michael Beckwith, D.D.

One Sunday morning a man approached the New Member Information table of the Agape International Spiritual Center seeking directions to where he was to later meet a man named Mark. "By the way," he continued, "do you know if Mark is here yet?" The question itself seemed ordinary enough, except that Agape's congregation is made up of 9,000 members with as many as 2,000 present at each of its two later Sunday services. "Oh yes, Mark is here," the helpful volunteer assured her inquirer. The man leaned in a little closer, as though to confide classified information. "I've never actually met Mark before…is he black, or white?" A quizzical furrow of the brow, a brief pause and her answer came: "Oh, that aspect hadn't actually registered with me, but I know he's here, and you'll enjoy meeting Mark because he's a wonderful person."

When the incident was shared with me, I inwardly smiled in recognition that my inner call to found a spiritual center composed of the "beloved community," as Dr. Martin Luther King, Jr., so aptly put it, had indeed been realized—a community wherein individuals are seen with 20/20 soul vision. This clear seeing penetrates to the individual uniqueness of a person, all the while appreciating how the Creator shows up wearing humankind's coat of many colors arrayed so beautifully as every race of people walking the planet. The diversity of cultures, shapes and sizes of peoples, genders, sexual preference—all are included in the all-embracing love of the Spirit.

To know that the door of Agape's heart is as wide as the world, that our umbrella is big enough for all to stand beneath its sheltering embrace is evidence that Dr. King's dream is alive and manifests anytime and anyplace where men, women, and children are recognized and treated as individual expressions of God—the Light that "lighteth up every man, woman, and child who comes into the world."

When Divine Love is our approach to life, 20/20 soul vision lights our way to a personal and global world of peace, harmony, and unity where our interconnectedness is honored and our diversity is celebrated. Our children indeed then become rich as they inherit from us a planet united on the highest vision for our human family.

May all of us seek to develop our soul's inherent 20/20 vision so that each of us may be a beneficial presence on the planet.

FOR OUR WORLD

Mattie J. T. Stepanek

We need to stop.
Just stop.
Stop for a moment…
Before anybody
Says or does anything
That may hurt anyone else.
We need to be silent.
Just silent.
Silent for a moment.
Before we forever lose
The blessing of songs
That grow in our hearts.
We need to notice.
Just notice.
Notice for a moment…
Before the future slips away
Into ashes and dust of humility.
Stop, be silent, and notice…
In so many ways, we are the same.
Our differences are unique treasures.
We have, we are, a mosaic of gifts
To nurture, to offer, to accept.
We need to be.

Just be.

Be for a moment…

Kind and gentle, innocent and trusting,

Like children and lambs,

Never judging and vengeful

Like the judging and vengeful.

And now, let us pray.

Differently, yet together.

Before there is no earth, no life.

No chance for peace.

Part IV

Chosen Children

⌒

Adoption is when a child grows into the tummy of one mommy, but is born into the heart of another.

—Author Unknown

"Our Angel"

Linda Darby Hughes

On a summer day in 1982, the call came. "Mrs. Hughes, it's Hazel Patterson, the director here at DFCS. How are you today?" Her deep, smoker's voice was tentative…apologetic. I was surprised; usually a caseworker called us.

"We have a newborn being placed for adoption. She'll need a foster home for 2 to 3 months while we handle formalities; if you can just see your way clear?"

I couldn't figure out the question mark. Our daughters would do handsprings! "Yes, we'd love to have her. When can I pick her up?"

"I should tell you, Mrs. Hughes, this child is black. I understand if you say no. We've never placed a black child in a white home before, but our only black foster home is full. We're at our wits' end here."

"We'll be delighted. How soon can we pick her up?"

In a haze of joy, I rounded up bottles and tiny soft things I hadn't bought in years, answering my daughters' questions: How little will she be? Can I feed her? Can she sleep in my room? What will she look like?

Knowing words can't describe a newborn; we drove to the hospital and pressed our noses to the nursery window, slack-jawed at God's finest work.

We brought her home in the same crocheted blanket that had wrapped both our babies. She was a tiny doll, with dark, looping curls framing a wrinkled face as pale as our girls' had been.

Awed, Karyn whispered, "Mama, what's her name?"

"She doesn't have one until she's adopted. They could assign her one. Or…," I smiled, "we can name her." The girls squealed in delight.

"Well, what shall we name you, little angel?" I kissed the wrinkled forehead and handed her to Melinda.

Melinda, 8, who spent her life gently cuddling dolls, kissed the soft curls and whispered, "I think we should call you Angel, like Mama said."

"Angel. It's perfect!" Karyn danced around, singing, "Angel, Angel, little Angel…Angel what, Mama?"

I thought for a moment. "Angel Ruth, I think. Do you remember the Bible story about Naomi and her daughter-in-law Ruth?" They did. "Remember how Ruth left her home and went with Naomi to a faraway place for the rest of her life? Well, our little Angel will leave her first home, here, one day. We'll love her as much as possible until then."

"Angel Ruth Hughes!" Karyn said, "It's perfect!"

Angel's every demand was our wish. We would do any silly thing to see a smile on that tiny solemn face.

When she was a month old, my husband, Johnnie, and I were in a restaurant near two other couples with babies. Johnnie was tickling Angel, coaxing one of those bubbly grins, when another baby started crying. He glanced over; then looked back at Angel with a frown.

He glanced around again, and whispered, "Their babies look pale. Don't let them close to Angel, they might be sick!"

Alarmed, I looked hastily over and then back at Angel. His frown deepened as I started laughing. "What's so funny?"

"Honey, they're not pale; they're white!" Wincing, he laughed with me.

We prayed often for the right parents for Angel, grieved that they would miss these precious weeks. But, we faithfully kept a photo journal for them, and had portraits made monthly. Once, a disgruntled clerk searched through jumbled portrait packets, complaining at the disorder. "Finally!" she exclaimed, as she slapped the package on the counter.

Then, as she saw the top picture, "Good grief! That's not *your* baby..." Suddenly her eyes dropped to Angel's stroller. Blushing, she stammered, "I must be losing my mind, forgive me. I guess her father's black, huh?" She gave an uncertain smile.

"Yes, I think so," I answered. "I know her mother is." She was still smiling when we left.

Angel was 19 weeks old when the agency called. A childless couple about 200 miles away had been waiting three years for a baby. They were coming to see our Angel.

The girls were showing Angel their best silly faces in a visiting room at DFCS when a petite, black woman peeked around the door, eyes shimmering with tears. Above her, a tall man smiled broadly. At my smile, they came around the door and he removed his cap.

The young woman clasped her hand over her mouth, closed her eyes for a moment, took a deep breath and took the baby. Angel studied her solemnly; then touched her cheek with one fingertip. The man wrapped the two of them in his arms.

Forgotten, we slipped into the hallway. The woman's soft sobs followed us out.

The couple was taking Angel to their hotel for a four-hour visit. If it went well, Angel would leave us the next afternoon.

But when we got home, they were already waiting. The girls ran to get Angel, not realizing what this meant. The couple couldn't even make it through a four-hour visit.

Karyn grabbed Angel. "Hey, Squirt! How ya doing, Angel Peanut!" Melinda followed, chattering as they went toward the house. Dread slowed my steps.

The woman's words tumbled over each other, "Mrs. Hughes...Linda,... we just couldn't wait! Tell us everything! What does she eat? What's her favorite toy? We're naming her Arletta, after my mother! She'll be so thrilled!" Her husband chuckled as she wound down.

I sagged to the porch steps, trembling. They wanted her! They couldn't wait! I felt foolish; of course they wanted her, she was absolutely perfect!

The next day we took Angel for a good-bye lunch. The young waitress, openly curious, finally blurted, "Your girls are so pretty...they all look just like their mother!"

When we screamed with laughter, her face flamed. I motioned to Karyn, who finally recovered enough to say, "It's OK, she's not ours. Her name's Arletta, and we're keeping her for someone else."

It was the first time we'd said it out loud; it felt right.

Our Angel left us later that day. The old crib and ruffled pink curtains went back in the attic. We put up red ones for the 8-year-old boy who would arrive tomorrow.

About a year later, I returned from errands to the girls squealing, "Arletta and her parents are here! They want to come over!"

Johnnie hurried home and we stood on the shady porch watching them climb our front steps leading a sturdy toddler in a pink sundress and matching hair bows. I knelt to meet that solemn penetrating stare I knew so well.

"Hello, Arletta," I said softly. She released her mother's hand and came straight into my arms. I stood and kissed her soft cheek. With palms against my shoulders, she leaned back to stare intently at my face. Then she reached out and touched my mouth.

"That child won't go to anybody," her mother said. "But I knew she would go to you."

"Her name's Arletta, but we call her Angel."

The Baby Flight

Paul Karrer

⌒

I had never held a deformed infant in my arms before. To tell the truth, I had never even seen an infant like this before. Now, here I was responsible for delivering three tiny orphans to their adoptive parents on Christmas Eve.

Twenty-eight years old, a New England Yankee through and through, I taught English on Cheju Island, Republic of Korea. College students all over the country had been rioting and had succeeded in closing colleges. I was fed up and needed to go home. One of my colleagues informed me of the "baby flights," whereby I could travel from Korea to the U.S. and back for a mere twenty-five percent of the normal fare. But there was a hitch. The traveler had to transport not one, not two, but *three* infants. That translated into at least three flight changes— Tokyo, Anchorage, and New York, in my case. I would have to bring diapers, formula, pacifiers, and much patience. The alternative was to pay the full fare.

I found myself boarding a plane with three infants, aged three months, seven months, and a year-and-a-half. They came complete with runny noses and wet diapers.

When the plane finally took off, the poor kids let loose with a terrible howl. As the plane climbed, it began to vibrate violently. In unison, all the babies quieted. A few seconds later, the plane stopped shaking and in unison the babies resumed crying.

The entire planeload of passengers burst into tension relieving laughter.

One thing gave me pause. The eighteen-month-old infant, who was as quiet as a mouse, had a massive head with disproportionately minute arms and fingers. Obviously, the poor thing was affected with dwarfism. I was surprised by my reaction. I was repulsed and I began to worry if the new parents on the other side of the Pacific realized what they were having delivered to them. I didn't look forward to the transfer, but was too busy to give it much consideration. Babies were hollering. The one on my lap was wet and the milk formula was low. I rapidly learned how to clean a wet bottom, put on a new diaper, and stick a pacifier in an open mouth.

Two American soldiers asked if they could each take a baby. I happily agreed, deluged by the needs of three little ones. So, I sat there alone, holding the eighteen-month-old baby with the very large head. I noticed her long eyelashes. As I looked into her eyes I couldn't help but see that they held a crisp, intelligent glow. Then she smiled and I was hooked. Funny how things like that can change you. From that point on, she radiated beauty, and she never left my arms.

In Tokyo the plane had a stopover. The soldiers apologized for not being able to help anymore as they had another flight. They each handed back a baby. I clung to *my* baby and proceeded to change the diapers of the two others. A pile of single dollar bills fell from their clothing. I quickly glanced at the departing soldiers. One of them gave the thumbs-up sign and blurted, "Little buggers gonna need all the help they can get. Merry Christmas."

Not many minutes later an attractive Asian woman approached.

"Twenty-four years ago I was one of those kids."

She took the noisiest child of the lot. During the flight she would show up and lend a hand, clean a bottom, or soothe an unsettled little one. She then took one infant, walked down the aisle and I didn't see her until the plane landed.

By now I had developed a strong bond with "my" baby. I even named her Tina. The more I thought about giving her to someone else, the more I worried about her prospective parents. *I feel like a slave trader and a traitor all wrapped into one.*

Finally, the plane landed. People rushed in, matched identification tags and off they sped with their new children. But I still held Tina, and it seemed like nobody was coming on board for her. In the end, I trudged off the plane to a small crowd. Tina clung to me tightly and cried.

Then I spotted them standing to the side of the exit. The man was no more than four feet tall, and his wife even tinier. They walked toward me and the small hands of the couple reached up for Tina. As I passed Tina, she said, "Oma" to him. That means mom in Korean. At that point I cried.

The next year I paid the full fare. The baby flight was too expensive.

GIFTS OF LOVE

Marie McBride

⟶

When Susan and Martin learned they could not bear children, their misery was so acute that it was a physical pain. For months, they lived in the twilight world of the half alive.

Yet soon, their courage and determination kicked in, and they made up their minds to adopt a baby—they could have a family!

The adoption process was a tough, head-to-head competition. Susan and Martin lived under a microscope for months. They revealed every detail of their lives—financial, emotional, physical, family background. Even though they were exhausted by meetings with their social worker and attorney, home visits and counseling sessions, they courageously pushed onward.

Their social worker, Mrs. Stevens, asked, "What kind of child do you want?" Susan and Martin answered, "A baby."

On Monday morning, a month later, Susan snatched up the ringing phone and took a deep breath of utter astonishment. "You have a baby for us!"

"Yes," Mrs. Stevens answered. "He's two days old—he's biracial."

"When can we get him?"

"Did you hear me—he's biracial?"

"Yes, when can we get him?"

"We fly to Tennessee on Wednesday. The teenage parents have already signed adoption papers, but the mother wants to meet you and Martin."

"Make the plane reservations."

Susan spent the next day in a state of controlled excitement. Even the air seemed to be holding its breath while she put fresh sheets on the crib and packed a diaper bag. She felt an electric sparkle—in two days, the rest of their lives would change forever.

"What if she doesn't like us?" Susan whispered to Martin on the plane.

"What's not to like?" he said.

When they arrived at the hospital, Susan and Martin sat outside the nursery while Mrs. Stevens talked to the birth mother. Susan's adrenalin level began to rise, and she twisted her hands nervously in her lap. Martin paced the floor, his hands shoved in his pockets, his shoulders hunched forward. "What's taking so long?" he asked.

At that moment, Mrs. Stevens and a teenage girl holding a baby entered the waiting room.

"Mr. and Mrs. Abbott, this is Lily," Mrs. Stevens said. "Let's sit down."

Susan's heart thumped against her rib cage. She could barely control her excitement.

Lily cradled her baby in her arms. Susan felt a lump in her throat when she saw the tears on Lily's pale face.

Lily spoke first, "I love my baby, but I can't take care of him. I'm fifteen and his daddy's sixteen. My parents won't let me marry the father because he's black."

Susan swallowed hard and bit back tears. She'd witnessed many painful scenes, but this was the worst.

Mrs. Stevens, sensing the tension in the room, said to Lily, "Mr. and Mrs. Abbott will be wonderful parents. They will love your baby with all their heart. Do you want to ask them anything?"

Lily, trying to discipline her voice to maintain control asked, "Would you send me pictures?"

Lily's request surprised Susan. Mrs. Stevens patted Lily's hand and answered, "It's up to them."

Mixed feelings surged through Susan—she had not expected further contact with this girl! *But she's giving us her child!* She suddenly felt a warm glow flow through her and said to Lily, "I'll send you pictures."

"Thank you," Lily answered. She kissed her baby and handed him to Susan. "Will you tell him that I love him very much?"

"Yes." Susan's hands shook as she took the baby. Slowly she pulled the blanket from around him. He was sleeping—a crooked little smile on his face. She lifted him to her breast and said, "Thank you, Lily." Smothering a deep sob, Lily left the room.

That night, the Abbott family—Susan, Martin, and Shawn returned to their home in Georgia.

Ten months later, Susan folded diapers in the laundry room. Shawn pushed his walker around the table, bumping into walls and doorways, "You'll be walking soon, sweetie," Susan said stacking diapers in the basket. "Push hard, Shawn! Come with me to the den."

The phone rang just as she entered the room. "This is Helen Stevens."

Susan panicked—had Lily changed her mind? *We can't lose Shawn!*

Hesitantly, Susan asked, "Why did you call?"

"Lily's pregnant again—the same boy. Her baby girl is due in August. She wants you to have her."

Susan gasped, "This is Shawn's sister!"

"Yes. Lily has a college scholarship and can't keep the baby."

"We've talked about adopting another child, but Shawn's only ten months old."

"I know. Why don't you and Martin talk about it and get back with me?

"Okay."

After Susan hung up the phone, she lifted Shawn from his walker and hugged him tightly. He giggled, babbled and put his arms around his mother's neck. Susan began to cry, and Shawn touched her cheeks with his fingers.

Susan and Martin talked until dawn. By the time the sun rose, they'd made their decision. "She's Shawn's sister. Now we'll really be a family. I'll call Mrs. Stevens," Susan said kissing Martin on the cheek.

"You're doing the right thing," Mrs. Stevens replied. "I'll tell Lily you'll take the baby."

Six months later, Susan, Martin and Mrs. Stevens again flew to Tennessee. As the plane prepared to land, Martin whispered to Susan, "I'm a little scared."

"Me too," Susan answered. "We didn't plan this, but it happened—now we have two gifts."

Lily looked different. She'd lost weight and cut her hair. She smiled when she saw Susan and Martin. Sitting beside them holding a tiny pink bundle, she said, "Mrs. Stevens sent me pictures of Shawn. He's beautiful."

"Yes, and he's mischievous and curious. He keeps us busy. Every day is an adventure," Susan answered.

Lily looked at the tiny girl in her arms. "She belongs with you and her brother. I'm going to college and make something of myself. I won't worry about my children—you're the best parents they could have."

"We'll take good care of them," Martin said, biting his lip to control his emotions.

Lily handed the tiny pink bundle to Susan. She hugged Martin and Susan and said, "Thank you!" and left the room.

Snuggling Alice in her arms, Susan whispered to her new daughter, "Just wait until you meet your big brother!"

WILDFLOWER IN A ROSE GARDEN

Shae Cooke

～

The rain pelted the living room window of our three-story walk-up. I pressed my face against the cold glass and mouthed words I don't remember—noiseless words meant for my six-year-old image of God. The sky streamed in through a crack, and I pressed closer, hoping my tears would flow through and blend with the rain. That way, Mommy wouldn't notice how sad I felt.

"If only Daddy wouldn't drink," I thought. "Then I could stay." I shivered, though not from the drafty window. They were coming to take me away. I unloaded a few sobs as the ten o'clock freight train thundered by in the near distance. I didn't want her to hear me cry—I promised I'd be brave.

A shiny blue car pulled up to the curb, and a slender woman slipped out. She wore a burgundy-colored suit, and her hair was as black as coal. She held a briefcase in one hand, an umbrella in the other. It might as well have been a broom—she was mean. On her last visit, she made us cry. My mother told me that this time, I had to leave with the lady.

"Mommy, she's here, she's here, don't let her take me!" I forgot all about my promise and wept. She scooped me into her arms and carried me to the makeshift sofa. She brushed aside an empty beer bottle and set me onto her lap.

"Shhh, Sparrow," she said. "It's for the best." She swept a stray lock from my face and pulled me close.

The doorbell rang and my mother rose to answer it. She and the social worker exchanged words, wrote something on a piece of paper, and then beckoned me. My mother handed the social worker a small, tattered suitcase and then knelt level with me.

"I'm planting you in a better garden," she whispered. "Be a good girl, and remember, I love you."

The social worker led me down the rickety stairs to the car. I resisted her hand, but she grasped me tighter.

I tumbled into the back seat with my suitcase. I wiped the fog from the window with my sleeve and looked for my mother. I couldn't find her.

We drove through the familiar neighborhood to my unknown destination. The social worker didn't speak except to let out an expletive as a group of teenagers hurled a water bomb at the car. We passed by my friend Jean-Luc's house—a dilapidated makeshift shanty.

We turned right, past Mr. MacGruther's corner store, and headed toward the train tracks. I'd never been on the "other side" before. As we crossed the intersection, it was as though we'd switched channels from black and white to living color. The sun broke through the somber clouds, and a kaleidoscope of new scenery zoomed by.

The homes grew in size the farther we traveled. Enormous dwellings tucked into wavy blankets of soft, green grass. Umbrella-type trees lined boulevards—their soft canopies like porticos to a lifestyle so foreign to me.

The car turned, and we wound our way up a large hill, past a school, and into a cul-de-sac. A woman with blond hair and a long, black coat waved at us, and we stopped. Her face had an expectant look, and her smile was as warm as a sunrise. She opened my door, took my hand, and led me out of the car. Her hands rested on my shoulders and she stepped back to appraise me. For a moment, my threadbare clothes and mussed hair made me feel self-conscious, so I drew back. I felt as gray as the sky I left behind. But that feeling lifted as I suddenly found myself lost in the unfamiliar folds of her coat. She held me close, and I breathed in the delicate scent of her perfume.

"You are beautiful!" she trilled. "Like a wildflower!"

She took my suitcase and then led me up the rose-trellised path toward the front door of the house. I stopped to touch a velvety pink petal—it was so delicate, and it emitted a glorious fragrance.

"That's a rose," she said. "Go ahead and pick it. It will look lovely in your room."

When I walked into the foyer, I felt small. It was larger than our whole duplex. A wide staircase led to the upper floor.

"My name is Mrs. Byers," the woman said. "You can call me Mrs. B if you like... ah, here's your room. I hope you like it." I stood transfixed. "There must be some mistake," I thought. "... Was it all for me?" There was a canopied bed in the middle of the room. Plump pillows held up an array of plush animals, atop a soft, lacy comforter. A mirrored vanity complete with hair-brush set and toiletries stood in the corner. On the other side of the room—a huge Barbie dollhouse, complete with furniture and wardrobes. The walls shimmered in a soft, blue hue, and sheer organza curtains shifted in the breeze of the open-paned window. And there, on the wide dresser, was a framed photo-graph ... of me and my family.

"I'll just leave you alone for a little while—let you settle in. Call me if you need anything. Oh, and by the way, I'm so glad you're here." I blinked back a tear.

I sat on the edge of the bed—and stared at the rose. It all seemed too perfect. How could I ever belong here? Everything was in stark contrast to what I knew.

As though reading my mind, the door opened, and Mrs. B came in with a vase full of the most glorious flowers I had ever seen.

"These are for you," she said and placed them on the dresser next to the photograph.

They were wildflowers, similar to the ones I used to pick for my mother, down by the train tracks: Queen Anne's lace and bellflowers, primroses and violets, daisies and larkspur!

"You grow these in your garden?" I asked with a tinge of excitement.

"Oh yes, I do," she replied. "They are such hardy flowers and grow wherever I plant them, and sometimes where I don't plant them."

I grew into my new life too, just as my mother planned. I discovered that if a wildflower could grow and adapt on either side of the tracks, so could I. Somehow, I think my mother knew that when she let me go.

Shortly after my mother's sudden death a few years later, Mrs. B and I visited the train tracks in the old neighborhood and planted a rosebush beside a cluster of Queen Anne's Lace growing there, as a reminder of my mother's gift to me of two worlds.

… And Mrs. B? She still cultivates her roses and plants new wildflowers from time to time.

Ebony and Ivory

Julie Wassom Melton

When they were growing up, our girls fell asleep each night to the tinkling of ivory keys as my husband played lullabies on the piano. His fingers made the Steinway sing soothing songs for our two girls, Anjali and Elizabeth. Anjali was born in India, and "came home" to us at five months of age. Elizabeth was born three years later, our first and only birth child.

In the Calcutta airport, Anjali was all eyes when the adoption agency representative placed her in my arms. Huge and brown as her skin, those five-month old eyes danced from person to person in the group of friends who had come to the airport to celebrate with us. I could not take my own eyes off this beautiful baby, overjoyed to have her as my daughter. When her glance caught mine, cultural differences vanished and her gaze seemed to say, "*Namaste*,* to my new mom."

We took Anjali everywhere, never concerned that she was dark and we were white. To us, we were simply a family unit. Anjali's jet black hair, round face, and snappy eyes drew admiration from complete strangers in the grocery store, on stroller rides in the park, and at neighborhood gatherings.

When she was in preschool, we moved to a new neighborhood, delighted to find that our next door neighbors were a mul-

---

Namaste is a Sanskrit word that means "I bow to the divine in you."

ticultural family. Our dreams of becoming a larger family were answered when I became pregnant and had Elizabeth. Fair and blond, her appearance was a noticeable contrast to Anjali's. When people would ask, "Are these both your children?" I would answer without hesitation, "Yes, we call them Ebony and Ivory. Aren't they precious?" After a relieving laugh, they all agreed.

As in most families, the girls grew through early childhood developing their own strengths and uniqueness. Anjali loved to sing, took voice lessons, sang solos at our church, and became a member of the school choir. Elizabeth learned to play the piano. When school friends would ask Elizabeth if Anjali was her sister, she would reply, "Yes, she's Ebony and I'm Ivory." Some thought those were their real names!

As teenagers, enmeshed in the sometimes cruel social world of high school, the girls become advocates of multicultural families. With a clear vision of the oneness of our souls, they embrace the new knowledge and perspective each cultural group brings to their experience. To them, color is nothing more than surface pigment. Character is deep, and far more revealing.

Now, our family seeks out opportunities to mix cultures, especially those of India and America. Thanks to having Anjali in our lives, we have all learned to see with eyes that dance to the music of Ebony and Ivory.

FRIEND OF MY HEART

Josie Willis

"What's wrong, Georgia? You seem down." I had arrived at the radio station early that morning to get a head start on writing ads for the clients. I had held the job as copywriter for only six months and was putting in fifty hours a week to produce commercials for both the AM and FM radio stations where I worked. Newly married and ambitious, I didn't mind the long hours. The advertisers were thrilled with my work, and as yet I had no children and could devote extra time to the job.

Now I searched Georgia's face for clues to my question. Was one of her boys sick? Was one of the salesmen harassing her again? The sales manager disliked blacks. His remarks to her often contained racial overtones. Even though his words cut deep, she seemed to handle him with grace and skill.

"Promise you won't tell anyone?" She twisted her hands nervously, looking around to make sure no one was listening.

What was it that could be so bad?

A single mother at twenty-four, Georgia had two energetic boys, Daryl and Desmond—normal kids who loved to play basketball and roughhouse with each other. Their father, eighteen like Georgia, deserted the family soon after Daryl was born. Georgia, determined to raise them right, juggled menial jobs to support the sons she adored. Yet she always found time for them, hoping to compensate for the loss of their father.

Finally, her hard work had paid off. She was offered a job as a news reporter at the radio station where I worked. It meant a substantial pay raise and more food on the table. She was proud she had accomplished so much on her own.

"I have Hodgkin's disease," Georgia said, jolting me back to the present. "The doctor said I have six months, maybe a year, to live." She struggled to keep her composure.

"Georgia, I'm sorry." I reached out to hold her. "Is there anything I can do?" The magnitude of the news made the question sound stupid.

"I'm not worried about me." She stepped back. "I'm worried about my boys. What am I going to do? Who's going to raise them when I'm not around?" Her voice went flat. "Their own father doesn't even want them."

"Let's talk about this later." I squeezed her hand. Some of our coworkers had arrived, interrupting our privacy.

That day, I couldn't concentrate on my job. I kept repeating mistakes in my copy.

"Are you feeling all right?" the sales manager quizzed me. I was usually fast and efficient, churning out copy by the reams.

"Yes," I pounced back, "just leave me alone." I was mad at him for Georgia's sake. Lucky for me I was white and didn't have to endure his racial remarks, as Georgia did.

She was so young, why did this have to happen to her? Why couldn't it be someone old. Then, guilt overcame me. Who was I to judge who should live or die?

In the months ahead, my husband and I invited Georgia and her boys to dinner frequently. I knew money was tight for her and that she would refuse any assistance. Having them to dinner was my way of helping.

"Your kids have such nice manners," I complimented her, and her face glowed.

There was a closeness between Georgia and her boys that was enviable. "I want them to grow up in a good home," Georgia said, "with someone who loves them. But who?"

In the next three months, she lost weight at an alarming pace. "This is a heck of a way to get a new wardrobe," she'd joke.

It hurt me to see her disappearing before my eyes. It made me painfully aware of the passage of time. If only there were something—anything—I could do.

"God has a plan for me and you, child," she said. "He gave us strength for our problems. Now you use that strength and get on with it." That was Georgia—tender, but tough. This was the friend I'd come to know.

"Georgia," I volunteered one night at our home, "what if we took your boys?" I held my breath, anxious for her answer.

Her face lit up as if the sun had sat on it. "You'd do that for me?" Her frail hands fluttered in her lap, and for the first time since she'd shared her secret with me, she cried.

Then quietly, she raised her head, motioning her children to her side. "Children, this woman is the friend of my heart." Then, looking away, she said, "I love you for offering, but I've decided they'll be raised by my mother."

My heart filled with sorrow. Despite her disease, she hadn't stopped fighting the battle.

"I thank you," she said, shifting her gaunt frame, "for keeping my secret. I thank you for being my one true friend. Problem is, the world has a long way to go before it changes, I think you know what I mean."

Time moved on, and Georgia with it, defying the odds. My husband and I were offered new jobs two hundred miles away.

Cheerful as always, she wrote me letters filled with the achievements and escapades of her two boys. A year went by, then two, three, with no word from her. I feared the worst, refusing to write to anyone who knew her.

Four years later, I received a letter from a former coworker at the radio station. "Georgia Curry just died. We were all surprised. Did you know she had Hodgkin's disease?"

"No," I wrote back, keeping my promise. "She was a wonderful mother and friend—even more, a wonderful person." I thought how, in death, as in life, she hadn't wanted to trouble anyone.

She had given me hope for my darkest days. I had given her light for hers.

AMY

Larraine R. White

We had never thought about adopting a child until 1984, when we met a couple who were selling their home. The wife introduced her children and said they were adopted from Chile. I suddenly knew, with a profound, intuitive, exciting feeling that our lives were about to change: We too were going to adopt.

At that time, adding more kids to our family was the last thing on our minds. Our lives were full with our two birth children, our son, J.D., age ten, and our daughter Alisa, age one. We were buying our first home. I was home schooling our son and dealing with a toddler, and my husband was searching for a new job. We didn't need another child. But I could not get the thought of adoption out of my mind.

Within three weeks, I had read twelve books on the subject. I called every agency in the DC area, ordered a subscription to *Ours* (a magazine about adoption), and inquired about FACE (an organization that gives courses about the topic). Every time I thought of not bringing a new child into our home, or tried to convince myself that two kids were enough, my hand would reach for the telephone and I would find myself talking to another agency. I knew there was a child out there who desperately needed us, and who was pulling us strongly to her.

We decided on Korea because we have always loved the country. We also decided to adopt a child Alisa's age, but we thought having two infants would be too much for us to handle. Having two babies was wonderful, but enough! Since Alisa was only a year old, we decided we would wait at least until she was two before applying.

During the next year, it seemed everywhere I went I saw Caucasian people with Korean kids. I had never noticed them before. It's like when you are in love, the whole world is in love. When you are adopting, the whole world is adopting.

I also spent the year earning enough money to pay $5000 in fees by having a day care program in my home. My program went well enough, though there were days when caring for five or six toddlers was enough to bring on insanity. Every time I felt like quitting, I reminded myself that every diaper change, and every nose wipe, was supplying the money to bring our new child to us.

In September 1985 my husband and I started our very informative and exciting FACE course and began the application process to Associated Catholic Charities in Baltimore. In early March our home study was sent off to Korea, asking for a girl who was one and a half to two years old. Six months later we got the call. "We have an eighteen-month-old little girl for you in an orphanage in Korea. Come in and we will tell you all about her." When we saw her picture we knew she was the one we were waiting for. Her name was Mi Hun and in the photo, she was sitting on a tricycle, had cropped black hair, puffy cheeks, and looked as if she desperately needed someone to hug her. Her father had died of an unknown illness, and her mother could not afford to keep her. We knew she was meant for our family. We named her Amy Dawn.

In July, word came that Amy had the chickenpox which would delay her arrival. I felt so sad that I couldn't be with her to take care of her. July 22 came—her second birthday. I wondered what her birth mother felt on this day and my heart went out to her.

A few days later, Amy's travel plans were confirmed: July 30 at 10:30 p.m., BWI airport. We felt a range of emotions: excitement, jitters, happiness, fear, and confidence. We were sure we could handle anything a two-year old threw our way. After all, we already had two kids. We were experienced parents. Right? *Wrong!* We had never experienced grief.

Amy's escort group missed their connecting flight in Chicago, so her arrival at BWI was changed to 1:30 a.m. We put three-year-old Alisa, and twelve-year-old J.D. to bed. We all tried to sleep but were too excited. At last midnight arrived, and it was time to go to the airport. My in-laws met us there to help take care of our kids while we focused on Amy. As I waited for the plane, I kept thinking, "Boy, this sure beats labor pains!" Little did I know that the difficult part would come later.

During the twenty-four-hour trip, Amy's escort had settled and soothed her, and when they came down the walkway, Amy was in her escort's arms. She did not want to let go. The escort quickly handed Amy to me and left.

Amy kicked and screamed to get away from me, calling "Oma" (Mommy) after the escort. She worked herself up so much that she got sick all over herself. In the rest room, it took all of my mother-in-law's strength and mine to change her into the extra dress I had brought along. Eventually, we got her into the car with all of us trying to calm her. Alisa looked on in fright. Amy fell asleep on the drive home and we all got to bed at 5 a.m.

The following day I woke Amy at noon to try to get her on our schedule. She looked at me and immediately shut her eyes and burst into tears. I think she hoped I would go away.

I carried her crying downstairs and put her on the rug. She looked around like a cornered animal, her eyes darting here and there. It was J.D. who got the first smile out of her and got her to eat some bread. She accepted me at meal time and allowed me to feed her, which I did for a week. She then attached herself to me and would not let me out of her sight.

There were times during the first two weeks when I wondered if I had made a mistake. Part of that was fatigue because Amy woke up every 45 minutes screaming "Oma." But I reminded myself how strongly I had wanted her and worked to get her here. I told myself that there must be something I needed to learn from this experience. Also, I kept thinking that if she was capable of grieving this intensely, she was also capable of loving just as intensely.

For the next six months Amy's tears came for other reasons or for no apparent reason at all. It was distressing for us to see her cry with eyes closed, fists clenched, completely shutting out the world, and unresponsive to any attempt at consolation. I knew she was grieving for her lost life, and I prayed each evening that she would eventually accept us as her family.

It has been nineteen years since Amy's arrival. The grieving is far behind us. In its place is a very happy, loving, spontaneous young woman. When Amy walks into a room, gloom disappears and the sun comes out from her inner joy. She is one of the most loving and giving persons I know. It makes her so happy to give and share with others. One of her teachers said, "Amy is the light of my class. She is so adorable I wish she were mine."

Today, when I look at Amy, I see myself reflected in her. She is so deeply and profoundly a part of me. She has taught me to love universally. It is easy to love children and bond with them when they physically resemble you, but in some ways, that is a very narrow ability to love. The absolute exquisite beauty of adoption is to enable us to transcend the physical resemblances so that we can see and love on a deeper level. Seeing myself in her has taught me to see myself in other people. Loving Amy has taught me to love other people, because we are all basically connected to each other through love. Having children only by birth cannot teach us that.

Those of us who get to adopt are very fortunate. We felt we had gained so much from Amy that, when she was six years old, and Alisa seven, we adopted nine-year-old Emilie Chandra Rose from Bangkok, Thailand. It was Amy who took her hand and helped her adjust to our American way of life.

Coming Home

Jimmi Ware

I sensed her insecurity
And somehow I still managed to make her smile
My new foster child

My dark berry Princess welcomed her
To our home
To help make it her own

She was hungry so I fed her soul
Provided love and a hand to hold
Gave her a shoulder, when she needed to cry
When she needed space, we never questioned why

She slowly opened up and began to shine
It simply warms this heart of mine
She shed the cocoon and learned to fly
She dances on air and leaps toward the sky

She gives me hugs from the depths of her heart
I know her canvas is a work of the Creator's art
She loves collard greens and pinto beans
And corn bread, like I said her soul got fed

When I look in her deep blue eyes
She knows how much I care
I'm her freckle-faced mama
Braiding her long blonde hair

She's no longer alone
And there is no place
Like "our" home

PART V

LOVE BEYOND BOUNDARIES

~

If you judge people, you have no time to love them.

—Mother Teresa

MEETING GRANDMA

Shirley Jackson-Avery

Found out who I was when I looked into her eyes.
Found out who I was and I was quite surprised.
How could this woman look so much like me but differ in age
and nationality?

My mama always told me I looked like my father's side.
Staring at this woman I knew she hadn't lied.
But I never knew my daddy when I was small and none of his
photos ever graced our walls.
And no one ever said that I was half white. I always assumed
that daddy was just light.
Still, someone should have told me how much so I'd mirror this
grandmother I didn't even know.

Today we'd finally meet after thirteen long years. But it took
my mother's death to make her finally face her fears.
Looking at her, I felt I knew, answers to questions that were long
past due. Thirteen years ago, when my daddy met my mama,
they had me despite all the drama.
Unfortunately, daddy died before I turned one but not before
Grandma
Disowned her only son.

She just couldn't believe he could love outside his race. To her everything, including love, had its place.

I stepped toward her and looked at her white face. Would she reject me, because of my race?

Grandma finally looked up and tears escaped her eyes. She fell in love with me quite by surprise. She stretched out her arms and held me tight. She didn't seem to care that I was part Black and part White.

After years of rejection, my grandma finally let me "in."
She found out that my color was simply skin.

ALPINE ENCOUNTER

Arthur Bowler

"*Guten Tag.*" I swallowed hard as I heard those words. I was meeting my future parents-in-law for the first time and couldn't speak a word of their language. Sitting in their home in a village in Switzerland, as my wife translated between English and German, I wondered what I was getting myself into. Their demeanor, typical of many Swiss, was reserved and formal, quite unlike the American reception my girlfriend had received from my family in Massachusetts: hugs, smiles, and first names. I wondered if I would be able to make the adjustment to her country.

If you have traveled, you know of the things other than mother tongue that separate one culture from another—table manners, driving styles, even ways of answering the telephone. Over the next few months, there were many moments of laughter. In broken German, I once ordered shaving cream for my sundae instead of the other more tasty kind. But there were also moments of hardship; times when I felt homesick and thought there were too many differences.

One day, feeling particularly discouraged, I left the city, took the train to the mountains and climbed one of the famous peaks. I intended to come to a decision that day in the Alps: stay or leave; adjust or give up.

All alone, looking out over the valley below, I was approached by a shy, soft-spoken teenager. In broken English, she told me of her birth in India and how she was adopted by a Swiss couple as a child. She also told me about growing up in her new country; the struggles she had with the language and culture as well as the taunting and prejudice she had faced because of her dark skin. As the sun set, she turned to go and plucked two of the famous edelweiss flowers, which she then handed to me.

"They look a bit different on the outside, but inside they're made of the same stuff. Like people," She smiled. And then, "I hope you stay here, Arthur. Good luck," and she was gone.

That day was over twenty years ago. I was able to adjust, not because I focused on the things that make us different, but because I focused on the things that make us the same: the love, compassion and hope that binds us all, no matter what our mother tongue or mother color. I learned the language, became a writer and a minister in my adopted tongue, and now even drive as crazy as any Zurich taxi driver. And when I feel discouraged about the human race, I open my dictionary to the word seele. Here, under the English equivalent "soul," I find the same edelweiss flowers, given to me so many years ago by a young stranger on a mountaintop. Then I whisper, "*Danke*, my friend."

STAR-CROSSED LOVERS

Randall Hardy

It was on Christmas Eve of 1984 that I first laid eyes on her. Becky had long straight black hair that framed her strikingly beautiful face and dark piercing eyes. Upon meeting her, I felt a spark between us that revealed recognition between kindred spirits, one that bridged the cultural gap between our origins.

She was Jewish, born in Tel Aviv, and well schooled in life's mysteries and eccentricities. I was born a Gentile, and still somewhat unchallenged in worldly matters. Over the following months, our relationship blossomed. She had a way of making me feel pretty special. Even the scent of her perfume kept me enchanted long after we had parted company.

One day, Becky asked me to have dinner with her family on the following Friday evening. Becky's sister, Sarah, who was working for me in my health practice and had introduced me to her sister, seemed a little distraught when I told her of the impending dinner date. I didn't know why I felt tension from her, but I did.

On Thursday, while I was thinking of what I was going to bring to dinner the next day, Sarah seemed to read my mind, and spoke something to me, very softly.

"What's that, Sarah?" I said. "I couldn't hear you."

"You aren't coming to dinner tomorrow night," she said, her eyes downcast and avoiding mine.

Assuming that she was asking me a question, I replied "Oh yeah, I am still going and I was just wondering what to bring and…"

"No, Randall. I mean you can't come. You are not invited. Becky asked you to come without asking my parents first…"

"That's OK," I said. "If it's inconvenient, we can do it another time."

"No, Randall, you don't understand. It's very hard for me to tell you this. There can't be dinner at my parents' home with you and Becky. Now or ever."

"Why, Sarah? Did I do or say something that offended…?"

"No. No. It was nothing you said or did. It's who you are and I can't say any more than that. I just don't know how to tell you, explain to you… and I feel really bad right now… you have to speak to Becky about this. She will be calling later."

I was stunned. Becky called later that day.

"What gives, Becky?" I asked. "Is it true that I am not allowed to come to your parents' place for dinner tomorrow night?"

"Yes, it's true."

"Why?" I asked in disbelief.

She said, "Because you aren't Jewish, Randall. They would welcome you into their home as a friend, but now that our relationship is more serious, they want us to stop seeing each other! I am so sorry Rand. Really."

Her words created an ache in every cell of my body.

"I don't understand Becky." I tried to hide the hurt in my voice. "Your mom and dad have been so great to me in the past."

"Randall. I know this is hard for you. They want to remain as your patients. They respect you as a professional and as a person. They like the fact that Sarah is working for you. They just don't like it that one of their daughters is in love with a Gentile."

I could feel her pain as she groped to find words to explain an ancient cultural reality, a concept that was so real for her yet so abstract and foreign to me.

When her parents came to see me for their scheduled appointments, they greeted me warmly. Once, I even did a house call for Becky's dad when he was too ill to come for an office visit, yet I was still forbidden to visit their home socially. I couldn't comprehend the paradox. I was angry and hurt. Fortunately, I was able to act in a professional manner and made an effort to see them as the good people they really are. I must admit that from time to time feelings of confusion and resentment seeped through no matter how hard I tried to cover them up, mostly when I was alone with my thoughts. The temptation to indignantly ask them to leave, to humiliate them as they had humiliated me often played out in my mind.

Although Becky had stopped visiting her parents for Friday night dinners (a special evening of family togetherness and prayer for people of the Jewish faith), hoping to pressure them into changing their minds, they wouldn't budge. It was hard for her folks to turn their backs on a code of tradition that had been supported for thousands of years.

I asked Sarah repeatedly, "Why do they still persevere in making things so difficult for Becky and me." I was pleading for her assistance, but I could see that it was of no use.

"It's just the way things are Randall. It's been this way for generations and my parents won't change. This may be hard for you to hear, but they really care for you. I can understand that it's difficult for you to believe that they can like you and still not want you as part of the family, but that's just the way it is. I am truly sorry for that."

My other Jewish friends affirmed this explanation to me. "Your predicament is indefinable and inexplicable, but there it is. Walk away from it. This is one situation that will hurt Becky more than you know if you push this too far. The separation and the dissention between her and her family is too much for her to bear."

About six months after Becky and I stopped seeing each other, her mom dropped by to see me at my office. She embraced me warmly as she often did, but this time she held me longer and tears filled her eyes. She expressed to me how sorry she was for all the hurt she and her husband had caused and said that perhaps they were wrong. She explained it was just a cultural assumption that one should never marry outside of the faith. Could I forgive them?

I melted inside. She was being genuine and her apology was heartfelt and real. Yes, one could say that it was easy for her now that her daughter and I were no longer together.

At that moment, however, all that mattered to me was that Becky's mother was sincere.

The Gift of a Lifetime

Andrew Dan-Jumbo

My story begins before I was born, when my parents first met. My father, Steven Dan-Jumbo, was a very well-known physician in Nigeria. My mother, who is Caucasian, met him in London, and they fell in love.

The obstacles they faced were simply unimaginable. They started courting in the early 1950s, at a time when people of color were not so welcome in England. Those were still imperial days for Britain, and the British empire had a number of foreign colonies. They brought in workers from the West Indies and Africa and South Asia because the English didn't want to get involved in what they considered to be menial jobs. All these workers flocked to Britain in droves, and suddenly the British were faced in their cities with lots of people of color, who were not really welcome. They were definitely considered to be second class citizens.

So my mother's family had a hard time initially accepting my father, who was black. He wasn't made particularly welcome, and it must have been very uncomfortable for him—and for them. This was a man who was in England to further his education, to become a doctor. But he was a highly educated man, very well spoken, fluent in several languages, and when my mother's family finally took time to get to know him, they realized that you couldn't measure a man by the color of the skin.

My mother is an extraordinary lady, and she's always chosen friends who are very strong people. So a lot of her white friends were very open-minded when she was dating my dad, and of course, England never had any kind of whites-only policy the way South Africa and some parts of the United States did. But living in London must still have been very difficult for them. They were so far ahead of their time.

I know that when my parents went to Nigeria, it was much easier there. Racism tends not to be reciprocated in most African nations. Europeans may tend to have a racial feeling toward the African in their country, but although Africans have far more reason to be angry—after all, their countries were colonized by the Europeans!—when my mother went to Nigeria, she was welcomed with open arms. The people there accepted her and her differences. If anything, the fact that she was white was to her advantage, and they treated her with even more respect. Unfortunately, the same couldn't be said of white folk in England and how they treated my father.

So my mother moved to Nigeria lock, stock, and barrel. She was completely committed to living there with my father, who was a dedicated doctor and a very prominent figure in Nigeria. They had a very privileged life and my mother's social life was terrific—she got invited to all sorts of government functions, and people were very warm and welcoming.

My father was running a small medical establishment with a fifty-bed hospital. This enabled him to give his family quite a privileged lifestyle. He owned several homes, and we lived in an enormous huge Colonial-style house. It was traditional back then to hire help to take care of the house, and we had several servants—stewards, groundskeepers, a cook, and a driver.

Domestic help positions were often considered to be a great opportunity for people who didn't have too many prospects. The average person couldn't afford an education, so they took whatever job they could. Working for a wealthy family was considered quite a good position, really.

But for my father, paying decent wages wasn't really enough. He was very high on education, especially because his grandfather had worked so hard to make sure that his kids had gotten an education. So he felt very much that even though our servants were only being hired to perform functions around the home, he still wanted them to be educated. I suppose he wanted to be able to communicate with them on an intellectual level, and he wanted them to be able to function better. But he also simply believed passionately in education. I think in that way he was very much like a Bill Cosby. I remember when I was a child, he said to me, "You're going to have to work harder than your classmates because you're living in a white man's world. So you're going to have to work harder than your peers to achieve the same things—but that's the kind of thing that makes you stronger." Hopefully, they do...

At any rate, my father saw to it that all our servants went to school. We had one young lad named Moses—I think he was probably 14 when he joined the household. He came on board to be a steward: to help around the house on various duties and ultimately, he became head steward and ran the house alongside my mum.

This was all several years before I was born, but I know that Moses became great friends with my brother, who was close to him in age, and my sister, too, ended up being very close with Moses. I've seen pictures of them playing with Moses. He was a phenomenal young man, full of life and energy.

My father was a very disciplined man who ran a fairly strict household, and he didn't take too much nonsense from people, but he was very fair, and he got tremendous respect and devotion from all the people who worked for him. Moses was actually my father's favorite, and my father saw to it that he in particular got an excellent education. Long after he and my family parted ways, he went on to get a degree, which is rare in Nigeria—most people couldn't afford it and still can't. They have to work to survive.

All this time we were living in Port Harcourt, in southern Nigeria, near where the oil fields were. I had been born in 1964, so I grew up in this huge home, with servants and so on—but then suddenly, it all came to an end. A civil war had broken out between the north, where the government was, and the south, where the oil was. It was a bloody campaign with lots of hand-to-hand combat, which resulted in lots of people having to flee.

I think my parents must have known for a while that the inevitable was coming. But I was three years old at the time and completely oblivious as to what was going on. One day, my brother and sister were pulled out of school, and we had to pack up just a small fraction of what we owned and try to get out of the country.

It was quite an escape. We were leaving right as the army was advancing: they were literally shooting at our car as we drove away. So many people wanted to leave that the airline had to make a choice—people or luggage. Of course, they chose people. So after taking only a fraction of our things with us to the airport, we had to leave even those few possessions behind. Instead, they put two people in each seat—one adult and one child. The adult might not even know the child, but the children had to be taken out.

It must have been a horrendous flight, filled with European women who had married Nigerians and who, like my mother, had hung on until the last possible minute. Our plane clawed its way into the sky, and we left everything behind—including my father. Dad, being a doctor, felt an obligation to stay behind and tend to the wounded.

The day after we left, my father realized that the advancing army was systematically slaughtering anybody they considered to be an intellectual threat. So he dismissed the household staff, including Moses, who headed off toward the east. No one could take very much with them, and what they did take had to sustain them for a long, difficult journey through the countryside. My father saw Moses go off, carrying one large box among his possessions.

My father, meanwhile, joined with two other doctors, a Filipino and a German, and together they traveled into an area that I would compare to the Everglades. In Nigeria they call it the River State, because it's threaded by a network of waterways— they call them creeks. During the rainy season the creeks swell up, and the only way to travel is by water. Through this swampy area they went, heading for Dan-Jumbo village, which was named for my family though many other families live there, too. But we have a very large family in that village, and as a young lad, my dad used to go there. So somehow he was able to find his way, and he brought the other two doctors with him, and they were able to find sanctuary there. And there they stayed for three or four months, waiting for the hostilities to die down.

I can't imagine what that must have been like for him—having a beautiful home and all these belongings that he'd spent years collecting—and then simply having to march away. In England, meanwhile, we didn't know if my dad was alive or dead, though we eventually got word that he was in Dan-Jumbo village. We knew he was safe there, because no army could ever bring heavy equipment through those swamps and waterways.

Finally, the war ended. But the country was in complete chaos, and my father's life wasn't much better. He was just trying to pick up the pieces, to deal with the fact that his house had been looted and partly destroyed. He was trying to make sense of all that—but he had no intention of returning to England. He was deeply committed to his country, and also, he was quite a big man there. In England, he would have been nobody, but in Nigeria, everyone knew him, everyone respected him. So he intended to stay.

If it hadn't been for us, I think my mother would have gone back to join her husband, but by this time my brother and sister were in school, and they needed to be enrolled somewhere. It simply wasn't realistic to send them to school in Nigeria—all the schools had been destroyed in the war, all the books, the whole infrastructure that the British had put in place, and there simply weren't the resources to rebuild it. Besides, all the teachers had left.

Father wanted my brother and sister to go into boarding school, but my mother took a firm stand on that. She wasn't about to let her children grow up without her. So my father realized that he'd met his match. My mother stayed with us in England, and my dad stayed in Nigeria.

I believe that was the best decision—but it was very hard. My father had difficulty getting money out of the country, and my mother had to work two jobs. We did have the help of my mother's brother, but it was a very humble upbringing. We lived in government housing, and had nothing but a smelly kerosene heater for the whole house. My clothes always smelled of kerosene.

We visited Nigeria on many occasions, usually for a month around Christmas or Easter. We tried to go every year but we didn't always manage that. But those visits made a huge impression on me that has lasted to this day, because every trip reminded ne of how hard it is to survive in a third world country. We saw beggars and lepers on the street who had to fight each day to find one more day's worth of food. I'd see children sleeping on the streets, and it made our home back in London seem grand.

I remember that my English friends would go on vacation to Spain or Italy, while I would go to Nigeria. We'd come back after our summer break, and they'd be telling all the usual types of tourist stories. My story would be about how I went to a supermarket in downtown Port Harcourt and saw a beggar who had leprosy standing outside. My father had given me some money to buy things while I was in Nigeria, but when I saw the beggar, I gave all my money to him. He was so overcome, he started crying, and I stood there and watched him cry. The money meant too much to him—but to me, it was simply foreign currency, and it was quite safe to give it away because even though we didn't have much money, I knew I could always get more from my dad. I watched the man with leprosy cry, and I wondered why people in Britain had so much while this man had so little.

But the most extraordinary visit took place when I was about twelve or thirteen. Somehow by this point, we'd reconnected with Moses, who'd made it through the war and was now doing fairly well. When he heard we were visiting, he took it upon himself to travel some two hundred miles plus in a country where travel can be difficult. You can't just grab a Greyhound in Nigeria—it's quite an ordeal to get from one place to another! But somehow Moses came to where we were staying, and we all had a great reunion.

That evening after dinner, Moses suddenly produced a box—the same box that my father had seen him carry away from our house all those years before. Moses presented the box to my mother, and we all wondered what it contained. My mother opened the box and began to weep.

What this man had done was simply extraordinary. On the day that it came time for him to leave his home and to flee into the countryside, rather than bringing with him some precious belongings that he might need for the trip, he had taken it upon himself to empty out all our photo albums and to cram all of the loose photos into this box. That's what he chose to bring with him on his flight—and that's what he brought to my mother now.

I don't think my mother even realized how much she'd missed those photos until she saw them again. We'd left so suddenly, and with so few possessions, that she hadn't taken a single picture. So she had absolutely nothing from that part of our lives—no photographs, no pictures, nothing to show for the fifteen years she'd been living in Nigeria, nothing to show for the first years of her children's lives. Moses had literally given her back her history, our history!

Even at the time, I was moved by Moses' gift. Today I understand more than ever what an amazing thing he did, because he gave me my history, too. Without Moses, I would never have known what my mother and father looked like back then, what my brother and sister looked like when they were little, what kind of house I'd grown up in, what the family dog was like.... Because of this man's extraordinary kindness and thoughtfulness, we had our past back, and none of us could keep from crying.

I'll owe Moses a debt for the rest of my life. This man had not only saved our photographs, he had held onto them for years, not even knowing if he'd have a chance to see us. And then when he knew we were in the country, he took it upon himself to bring them all that way. If I ever have children, I will definitely take them to Nigeria. The people are such gracious people, such amazing people. With all their hardships—and they're part of the two-thirds of the world who are living in abject poverty—they still manage somehow to put a smile on their faces. With all his hardships, Moses had managed to give me and my family the most extraordinary gift, a gift we can never match, but that will forever be remembered. Thank you, Moses!

I think the biggest lesson I've learned is to appreciate what I have. There will always be someone who has more than I do and who might seem more fortunate—but visit a Third World country and your whole perspective changes. Suddenly owning a ten-year-old car doesn't seem so bad anymore.

I remember hearing the tale of an astronaut who noticed from up in space that when the world is viewed as a whole, you can't see any physical barriers. There are only the imaginary ones we create. I think we should embrace our fellow residents who are also citizens of Planet Earth. We are all just really lucky to be here!

UNDERNEATH WE'RE ALL THE SAME

Amy Skirvin

He prayed—it wasn't my religion.
He ate—it wasn't what I ate.
He spoke—it wasn't my language.
He dressed—it wasn't what I wore.
He took my hand—it wasn't the color of mine.
But when he laughed—it was
how I laughed, and when he cried—
it was how I cried.

LOVING LEVI

Diane Haldane-Doerr

I met him the summer after my fifteenth birthday. His name was Levi, he was sixteen, he was beautiful, and I adored him. Today, twenty-three years later, what I remember most about him is his smile. When he grinned, as he so often did, I was unable to keep from smiling myself, no matter how hard I tried.

We met when my brother started working in a summer program that was funded by the state. My brother was deaf, and I was hired to act as his interpreter in a weekly class held for all the work participants. Levi was in that class, and soon all I cared about, though, was getting through the week to Friday—when I would get to spend the day with Levi.

Fifteen is a tough age for most girls, but especially for me. I felt gawky and ugly and far from talented or special in any way. Except when I was with Levi. We spent hours talking, laughing, joking, getting to know each other. He made me feel that I was really worth something; that I was funny and pretty, smart and talented—special. He was kind, sensitive and sincere, handsome and riotously funny—beautiful in every way and unlike any other boy I knew. It was a while before I realized that the friendship I had begun to treasure was turning into something more. When I came to understand that Levi liked me a lot, more than just as a friend, I got a little scared. When I realized

I liked him that way too, I got really scared. What should have been an exciting and sweet time in my life turned into a period of distress. You see, Levi was black. I am not.

I was raised in a conservative house, and though my parents truly believe that you should give each individual a fair turn, that you shouldn't judge people based solely on appearance, they also firmly believe that interracial dating and marriage is wrong. And though I was taught this from childhood, I never believed it myself. But I did, and do, love and respect my parents, and I knew that if I challenged their beliefs, there would be a price—a price I wasn't willing to pay at fifteen years old.

So I kept going to the Friday classes, excited to see Levi and sick at the notion that one day I was going to have to face the monster gnawing away at my heart. That day finally came. Levi sat beside me on a bench in the hallway and, smiling all the while, asked me out on a date. I looked into his lovely brown eyes, so much darker and warmer than my own blue ones, and I said no. A million phony reasons ran through my mind but I felt I owed it to this wonderful boy to be honest. I told him I couldn't go out with him because he was black and because my parents, truly good, kind people at heart, wouldn't approve. I told him that I didn't agree with them, but I couldn't disobey them either. I said I was sorry and that if I could change the situation, I would. I thought he might get angry, but he didn't. He just looked sad. So very sad. And he told me he understood. I don't know if he really did, but I vowed that day never to cause anyone else the hurt I saw in his face at that moment. I hated myself for not being strong enough to stand up to my parents and say, "No, you're the ones who are wrong!" And I carried that self-loathing with me for a very long time. It still makes me sad to know that I hurt him so deeply, and I'm sad for myself too—

that I never got to know him better, that I never gave myself the chance to love him even more than I already did.

Over the years, I have thought of Levi often. Knowing him and loving him affected me tremendously and impacted the way I see my world and the people in it. I grew up and eventually married a man, who, though not black, is brown-skinned—born to Mexican parents. My daughter is also brown, and when she was a baby, a woman in the grocery store asked me where she came from, assuming that a child with such dark skin could not be mine biologically and, therefore, must have been adopted.

I don't know what happened to Levi. I don't know where he is today or if he is successful or happy. I hope he is. I suspect he is. And I hope that if he ever thinks of me, it is not with sadness or anger. I want to believe that I affected him in some positive way; I need to believe it, because I know he made me a better person. If I saw him on the street tomorrow, I would take his hands in mine and say thank you—thank you for changing my life and making me understand how beautiful this world can be when you see it with your heart and not your eyes. I know this wouldn't be much but, somehow, I think for Levi anyway, it just might be enough.

"TWO CULTURES, ONE WORLD, ONE HUMANITY"

Eric Anthony Ivory

My wife is Japanese. She did not have a choice of being born in Japan, or to be born Japanese for that matter, just as I did not have a choice of being who I am. When we fell in love, we decided it would be a good idea for me to meet her mother. My fiancé and I agreed that she would leave one week earlier to prepare her mother for our meeting. I was to arrive in Japan the following week.

When my fiancé arrived in Japan, she learned that her grandfather was in the hospital, ill from old age and years of hard work. Arrangements were made for me to stay at a nearby hotel, and my fiancé and I agreed to meet daily, or as often as we could. It was going to be difficult with her grandfather being ill. She had a responsibility to her family to help care for him.

When we asked my future mother-in-law to meet with us, she refused. She told her daughter that all the attention and focus should be on the grandfather. I was sad and hurt—deep down, I felt she wouldn't meet because I was a "Kokujin," a black person. The news media in Japan portrayed black people as entertainers, athletes, or criminals. I felt my own future mother-in-law also harbored this stereotype.

As our trip came to an end, I rode the train to Narita International Airport in Japan. My fiancé and I had agreed to meet at a particular restaurant inside the airport building. When I arrived, I was surprised to see my fiancé's mother and brother sitting at the table. We were introduced, but my fiancé's mother refused to look at me. Our first meeting lasted less than thirty minutes.

I was happy to have finally met my fiancé's family, but I was sad that her mother would not look at me. I was angry because I was, and I am, as much a human being as she. I am very proud of who I am. Yet, to her I was just a "Kukojin," a black person.

Next year, we flew to Japan together. I stayed at the International Youth Hostel in Tokyo. After four nights at the youth hostel, my fiancé informed me that her mother had agreed to allow me to stay in her house for two nights.

Well, those two nights turned into seven nights. My fiancé's mother saw that I knew a few Japanese words, loved Japanese food, and could use chopsticks as well as she. From that moment forward things changed. It was like night and day. I believe she began to see the common human spirit. Slowly, the years and layers of stereotypical thought began to fall away.

Today, my mother-in-law sees me as her son-in-law, a human being, who had no choice as to the ethnicity of birth. I am Eri-san (Eric). She speaks of me fondly as a member of the Tamura-san family. I am welcomed in her home and she prepares my favorite Japanese food and buys my favorite Japanese beer. My visits have grown from seven nights, to three weeks or more. I am still a "Kokujin," a black person, and I will always be, but her perspective of this word, and of our world, has changed to a positive one. We still have two cultures, but one world, one humanity, and now one family.

KOREAN KISSES

Paul Karrer

My daughter Amber is a *tiggie* (rhymes with *biggie*). Stripped to its essence, *tiggie* is a Korean word meaning nonperson, animal, or mixed race. Amber is Amer-Asian. Her mom is one hundred percent Korean, and I am one hundred percent Anglo. That anyone could hate my child because of her gene pool is beyond me. But in the end, *tiggie* has the same gut punch value as does the "n" word.

Eighteen months after our daughter's birth, my wife Mi-Ra and I decided it was time for her to mend the family fence and go back to Korea. We had, after all, eloped and brought a *tiggie* into the world. Would the two of them be accepted? I could not make it back with them because of my job, but I wanted to protect them from what Mi-Ra and I had suffered in Korea. However, even in multicultural California, things had not turned out too well for the three of us.

Monterey, California, harbors a world-class bay and Steinbeck's Cannery Row, but even near flowing tides of opulence, ignorance can run deeper than the submarine canyons hidden below the choppy waves. In an Asian store, Mi-Ra had our Amber bundled on her back, Korean style, allowing freedom of movement for the mother. Mi-Ra politely waited in line to check out a twenty-pound bag of brown rice. She smiled with rosy cheeks, basking in the glow of contented motherhood. Two ancient Korean grandmothers shuffled behind her, stopped, and whispered, "*Tiggie, tiggie, tiggie.*" A shattered Mi-Ra told me this later.

If this happens in the USA, my god, what will happen to the two of them in Korea? It made me reflect upon our own Korean incidents during the years before we were married. Like the time two middle-age drunks staggered behind us as we walked the wharf of Pusan. I heard a thump. Mi-Ra winced.

"What was that?" I asked.

"Nothing," she replied as she stopped and rubbed her ankle.

I faced her sideways as two guys behind us barged past. One of them snarled. "One of those morons kicked you, huh?" I said.

"No," she lied.

"Which one?" I demanded.

"Don't make trouble. There are two of them. They'll kill you."

"They're drunk. I'll kill them."

"And the police will arrest *us*!"

That was the first time.

Twice I was jumped in the center of town as hundreds of people walked by. Dressed in my suit, briefcase in hand, I was walking to my university job, when, from behind, an arm grabbed me around the throat and wrestled me down. As I lay on the concrete, I watched a crazed old woman gesturing in all directions and screeching like a wounded banshee. An old lady had tackled me! Another time it was an old man. Sure they were crazies, but why me? Foreign devil, that was why! And now my child would head back to that kind of mentality.

But the worst of it was Mi-Ra's family. Her father had died long ago and her five brothers ruled the roost. Once, her third brother had spotted us together before anyone knew we were dating. The next day I didn't recognize her. Her lovely head was the size of a pumpkin. A purple bruise underlined her left eye. She walked with pain.

"What happened?"

"Bus accident," she lied.

"Did you go to the hospital?"

"Yes. Many people did." She lied again.

Years later, after that brother had a stroke, she finally told me what happened: Her brother had seen us together in the town market. He figured she'd dishonor the family by getting pregnant. Then the white devil would abandon her like so many had done during the Korean War. Then she'd have a *tiggie*. So he beat her, kicking her in the stomach and pummeling her face.

Now she was returning home ... with a *tiggie*. So I was worried.

The phone connection wasn't that good. It crackled, and there was a time delay. But I didn't care. "How's the flight?" I asked as the acids in my stomach stormed.

"Long."

"How did Amber do?"

"O.K., but she has a cold, I think."

I couldn't stand it anymore, "So what's your family's reaction? What did your mom say?"

"They think Amber is beautiful." Mi-Ra's voice was calm. I almost believed her.

"You're not lying this time?" I asked.

"No, I swear by the gods."

That was good. *I swear by the gods*. That was our private code. It meant the statement made was a truth to be believed at all costs.

"By the gods?"

"Yes, by the gods. My mother is holding her now."

"What about brother number three?'

"He has apologized many times. He bought Amber lots of presents. A gold bracelet and a gold ring. Korean twenty-four carat gold, not American eighteen carat," she added. "He cried."

"I still think he's a bonehead and I want to kick *him* in the head."

"Since his stroke, he can't walk anymore. These are not good thoughts."

"What else is going on?"

"Oh, you will like this. I walked in the market today with Amber strapped on my back, and a street shoe vendor begged me to leave her with him."

"Why?"

"He said she is so beautiful that people would stop to praise her and buy many shoes from him."

"Hmmm … I'll call you in a few days. Sah Rang Hae. Give Amber a kiss for me. Say hi to your mom."

"Sah Rang Hae. Call in three days."

This time, the connection was a little better, no crackling, but still a time delay.

"So how's Amber?"

"She has a cold, but a funny thing happened because of that."

"She's sick and a funny thing happened?"

"Yes, listen … yesterday I took her to the market strapped on my back. She sniffled and sneezed. I felt a strange movement and turned around quickly. A young businessman had a tissue and he was trying to clean Amber's nose. He turned bright red when I caught him. I think things are changing here."

"A businessman, huh. You're not drinking sake, are you?"

"Sake is Japanese. This really happened."

"O.K., you were drinking Maek-ju," I teased.

I knew better. She didn't drink.

"Oh … here is another one. Today in the market a group of high school girls kept on following Amber and me from a distance. Finally one of them ran up. 'Here, auntie, we bought a bag of candy for your beautiful baby.' They all smiled and ran away."

"You aren't making this all up to make me feel good?" I asked.

"It is all true. I can't make it up."

"Mi-Ra, I'll call in three days. Same time. Sah Rang Hae."

"Sah Rang Hae."

The third time, the connection was great. Not even a delay.

"Mi-Ra, how's things?"

"I think I'm going to cry."

The blood rushed to my face and a quick nausea nailed me.

"To heck with Korea! Come home now."

"No." she whispered, "No, it is good. Amber and I were in the market for a long time. I was really busy. After three or four hours of shopping I went home. Amber sleeps most of the time when I shop. When I took her home, I unstrapped Amber and I saw it."

"You saw what?"

"A kiss."

"A kiss? How can you see a kiss?"

"A red lipstick kiss. Somebody in the market kissed her. I don't know who."

I was quiet for a while, "You want to stay longer, huh?"

"Can we? My mother is very old now. Your *tiggie* is safe."

"I suppose. I'll call you in three days. Sah Rang Hae, you two. Hi to your mom." I said.

"Sah Rang Hae." She replied.

"Mi-Ra… say hi to that *bonehead* brother too."

THE THREE WHY'S MEN

Beverly Tribuiani-Montez

And then there are the three who married *into* our family: the convict, the cowboy, and the workaholic.

"Mere titles," I assured my boyfriend at the time (he's now my husband). "That's just the way my dad is. He likes to categorize things *and* people." Even I knew that what I just said made absolutely no sense. "He's harmless." I said with a reassuring smile. But the irritated expression on my boyfriend's face didn't change.

"Why does he think I'm just a dumb cowboy? Your dad doesn't even know me."

At the table that night, I could feel the weight of my father's disapproving stare. He was being quiet, which is a dead giveaway that he is in deep analysis of character. I could tell he was uneasy by the presence of an "intruder," whom he observed relentlessly. Did I mention that Marty's Portuguese, not Italian?

"Finally," whispered Rich, my brother-in-law, "the convict." Did I mention that he is Mexican and Chinese, not Italian? Marty looked at him curiously. Rich leaned toward him and whispered, "It's all on you now, buddy," he said, both relieved and mockingly. "The disapproving stare is finally off of me and on you." The two of them laughed, in spite of themselves.

My sister Jacqui and I looked at one another and laughed, too. These men had no idea the hoops they would need to jump through in the near future: attending family functions, birthdays, holidays, and especially last-minute get-togethers. And don't forget the respectful greetings and long and drawn out good-byes that take place at each and every gathering. Why, besides good food and loud conversation, big hellos and long good-byes are a must in Italian families.

Oh, and they would have to buy a suit, too.

"What man doesn't own a suit? Why don't they have suits?" My mother would say.

Well, a convict and a cowboy are two good candidates.

Bob doesn't have it so bad. He is my oldest sister, Ana's, husband. He is tall, handsome, a successful businessman and has no police record to speak of, and he's Caucasian. But, you have to understand my dad; there are no winners when it comes to men and his daughters. So, he had to give Bob some sort of fatal flaw.

"He work too much. All he care about is the work." My dad said one day to my sister.

"Is that it?" I thought to myself. Lucky.

Of course, Marty was the "cowboy" because he lived on a five-acre ranch in what my dad considered "the dirt," in Brentwood, California. And so what if he liked the smell of horse manure and preferred camping in the wilderness, as opposed to staying at a hotel resort.

Rich, was deemed the "convict" because ten years ago he spent a brief amount of time in jail for drugs. However, he has since completely turned his life around and is a hard working professional and a dedicated and loving husband and father.

These details don't have any relevance to my dad. He just calls them as he sees them and feels justified in doing so.

But I think that even my dad will admit that these three men have brought a lot of love and happiness to our family: a total of six grandchildren so far, strength and stability within our own families, and a view of the world outside of our own. Over the years, as a culturally diverse, happily dysfunctional, three-generation family, we have faced many obstacles and triumphs. We've driven across cities in the middle of the night to witness babies being born. We've carefully planned surprise parties, family vacations, bridal showers and funerals. We have waited in quiet sorrow for test results, sat for hours beside hospital beds, and have passed down cribs, high chairs, and much needed advice.

We have learned a lot from each other. From them, we've learned that you don't have to be Italian, you don't have to pretend to be perfect, and you don't have to make the right decisions all the time. You don't have to attend every family function. You don't need to politely laugh at the *"Portagee"* jokes, the "Chinese" jokes, or the jokes being told about you in a language you can't even understand. You don't have to justify your past or perfectly plan out your future, and you don't need to pretend that everything is great when you feel as if your whole world is caving in.

They too have learned a lot from us. They have learned that once you become a part of our family, you are surrounded by people who will love you, support you, pray for you, dance with you, laugh with you, cry with you, believe in you, yell at you, and be there for you no matter what. But, one thing will never change; you absolutely, positively, must own a suit.

Danny

Abby Warmuth

"Hi, Dad!" Danny said to my father as we walked by the family room. Danny had lived in many foster homes and called every adult male "Dad." He was absolutely carefree. We were four years old, we loved to giggle, make "muddy-gush" pies in the sandbox, put on plays in the backyard, and, I'm embarrassed to admit, moon the neighbors and then run like crazy. We thought this was hilarious.

I could spend all day playing with Danny. And many times I did. He was living with my next door neighbors and we'd frequently go to one another's house. I'm not sure what led to Danny being placed in a foster home. He was really happy, which I hope is an indication that it wasn't anything too bad.

We'd stand outside each other's houses calling "Dan-ny! Dan-ny!" or "Ab-by! Ab-by!" until the other one came out to play. Danny was my best friend. He absolutely glowed with joy. And whenever he was around, I was joyful too.

It was the early seventies, and we lived in a white suburb of Detroit largely populated with people who'd bitterly fled Detroit due to the race riots of the late sixties. When I begged my dad to let me drive with him to the corner store, I insisted that Danny come along too. This was a political risk for my father, who had a job with the city and drove a city car. But we didn't think anything of it. And if our neighbors did, they never said anything about our friendship.

One day, Danny was taken away. I didn't understand it. I was outside and heard Danny crying, "Abby! Abby! Abbbbbbbby!!!!!!" He was crying and trying to run toward me. My dad held me back and some people I hadn't seen before held Danny. The man and woman stuffed him in the back seat of a blue car and I could see his face and hands pressed up against the glass. My dad held me as I struggled to run after the car that slowly drove away, sobbing. I never saw Danny again, but I was told he had been adopted.

My father once said, "Danny didn't know that he had any black in him." Well, I didn't know I had any "white" in me. I don't know at what age people "know" these things, but I wish we never did. Even though it's been almost thirty years since Danny drove away in that navy blue car, he made an impression on me that my heart will never forget. He was someone who I loved completely and without reserve. Just thinking about losing him still makes the four-year-old in me cry. But now I also cry with happiness that Danny had a chance to have his own parents and one man called "Dad." Danny, I hope and pray that your adoptive parents were good to you and that you've had a wonderful, wonderful life.

JUST ANOTHER DAY

Cheryl Costello-Forshey

It was just another morning, it was just another day
As I headed to the local park, to watch the children play
For their laughter brought me pleasure, their giggles made me
 smile
And happiness was something, I hadn't felt in quite a while
And there beneath an oak tree, I sat upon the ground
My knees pulled up against me, shade flowing all around
As I felt my heart grow heavy, and sorrowful thoughts begin
Thinking of my daughter, tears dropping from her chin
Crying out in anguish, begging me to see
How much she loved her boyfriend, how their love was meant
 to be
But I only saw his color, the difference of his skin
And though I felt I wasn't prejudiced, I didn't want my child
 with him
And so I refused to listen, as she spoke to deafened ears
And instead of reaching out to her, I ignored my daughter's tears
I hoped it was a phase, a stage that she'd go through
For she was young and innocent, she didn't know the things I
 knew
How much her life would suffer, all the struggle and the pain
For the world would not accept them, they'd be forced to live in
 shame

But she didn't want to hear me, she claimed I didn't care
She said that I was close minded and that I wasn't being fair
So it was just another morning; it was just another day
When my daughter hurried to her room, threatening to run away

And there beneath an oak tree, I wiped away my tears
And thought about what I'd sacrificed for my daughter all those
   years
How I gave her independence, taught her to be strong
To find her way in the world, a place where she'd belong
And how she quickly turned against me, refusing once to see
That love is never blind, and some things aren't meant to be
And as I sat there self-absorbed, wondering what to do
Praying for God's guidance, to somehow get me through
I heard the sound of giggles, and turned to see at play
A little boy and girl in the park there on that day
Running near a maple tree, a recent storm had toppled down
With its large and sprawling branches, touching to the ground
Branches so inviting, for little boys to climb
And that's exactly what he did, leaving that little girl behind
For her legs were not as long, her hands were much too small
And every time she tried to climb, she'd quickly slip and fall
But she was quite determined, to overcome her plight
As she reached to claim another branch, to climb with all her
   might
And as her little dimpled face, broke into a grin
The little boy reached out his hand, to help his troubled friend
But he wasn't quite strong enough, though he did the best he
   could
So instead of climbing onward, he did what a true friend would
He let go of her little hand and then ascended down

And instead of climbing that tree alone, as one they walked
    around
And as I took a cleansing breath, turning I stretched to stand
Taking one last look at those two children, giggling and hold-
    ing hands
One whose skin was dark, the other whose skin was light
Together who'd found a way, to overcome their plight
Not caring about their differences, or the pigment of their skin
Instead working together, reaching out as friends
And it was there in that moment, watching those two children play
That my daughter's words came back to me, enlightening me
    that day

"Mom someday you'll see it, inside we're all the same
We each know how to feel, shed tears, and suffer pain
And yes our colors differ, but God created them with love
Wrens and robins both are birds, but their colors vary from a
    dove
And it was God who made those colors, to blend on earth as one
He gave us day and night, the moon, the stars, the sun
And one without the other, has no valued worth
It's because of our distinctions that we have merit on this earth
Butterflies and birds, flowers in the spring
In their different colors, to this world such beauty bring
So we have a choice in life, we each can choose to see
The differences in our skin, or what God meant for us to be
An array of different colors, the stars, the moon, the sun
And one without the other will make the world come undone"

It was just another morning; it was just another day
As I hurried home to hold my daughter, and ask her please to stay

To tell her how much I love her, and at last I understand

It's not our colors that make us different; it's how we treat our
fellowman

For God invented colors, to blend on earth as one

He gave us day and night, the moon, the stars, the sun

And though they all are different, they have purpose on this
earth

And one without the other, has no valued worth

PART VI

CREATING THE
BELOVED COMMUNITY

In a sense the concept of "us" and "them" is almost no longer relevant, as our neighbors' interests are ours as well. Caring for our neighbors' interests is essentially caring for our own future.

—The Dalai Lama

Arctic Jewels

Shinan Naom Barclay

As the aircraft skidded to a stop on the icy runway, I stared through the window at endless tundra, frozen white. Shivering, I climbed out of the six-seater bush plane and shuffled across snowy ice toward a figure in black. Taking my outstretched hand and wilting bunch of daisies, Father Vinchenzo introduced me to a group of Inuits. Their round faces, ruddy cheeks, and smiling black eyes warmed me in that deep-freeze land.

Three months earlier, while browsing my college's paper, I had read an ad: "Arctic Priest Seeks Volunteers." My excitement grew as I read about setting up a preschool, teaching catechism and mentoring teenagers in an Inuit mission fifty miles above the Arctic Circle. I immediately made arrangements to meet with Father Vinchenzo, a Jesuit priest from Italy, now pastor of Saint Michael's Arctic Mission.

The following week, at a formal interview, Father Vinchenzo told me long stories about the rigors of Arctic life. "The pay is ten dollars a month plus room, board, and round-trip transportation." He studied my reaction; I was undeterred. We chatted about my accomplishments. He closed my file with a "hmm," then looked up at me. "Shinan, I feel that you have a calling to my mission." I learned afterward, that no one else had applied.

Three months later, with the warmest clothes I could find, I flew to Fairbanks, then on to Kotezebue, fifty miles above the Arctic Circle.

*   *   *

Within two weeks I got the preschool started. Ten boys and girls, ages three to six, came to play, sing, listen to stories and learn their ABC's. In the mission's all-purpose room, I stoked the wood stove and watched snow crochet patterns of fine lace against the windowpane. The temperature had dipped to ten below zero; with twelve-mile-an-hour winds, the chill factor had plummeted to fifty below.

*   *   *

During the following months of Arctic darkness, I resigned myself to the cold and stood outside my cabin, watching the aurora borealis light the night sky. One night, my eighty-five-year-old neighbor, Edna Kobuk, joined me. "Hello," she smiled, showing mere stumps of teeth. Used as tools to soften hides for the mukluks of her eleven children and forty-seven grandchildren, her teeth were worn to the gums. We stood silent together, marveling at the flowing arcs of multicolored light. She gestured toward the brilliant aurora borealis. "Dancing spirits," she murmured, "the bridge to Jerusalem."

Nothing in my experience had told me that spirits dance and I had heard Father Vinchenzo preach to the teens that dancing can be an occasion of sin. Yet awed by the Northern Lights, I whispered to Edna, "If those dazzling lights are spirits, then I want to dance with them."

*   *   *

On Saturdays I shuffled to the Trading Post to check the mail and to visit with the villagers. They came not to buy or sell, but to warm, to talk, and to watch the elders who danced, chanted, beat the drums, and told stories to youngsters whose eyes glazed over at the sight of doughnuts, soda pop and candy.

Mail came sporadically on the bush plane but one Saturday, a letter arrived from my mother. Always curious for news about the lower forty-eight states, Edna asked, "How is home and your family?"

"My mother is fine," I told her, "but Mom says that my little sisters are sick with measles." For the moment I had forgotten that an epidemic of measles in the late 1800s wiped out thousands of Eskimos because they had no natural immunity to white man's diseases.

"Ah," Edna replied, then walked away. Several hours later a knock at my cabin door revealed Edna, the muskrat tail ruff around her parka frozen with tiny icicles. "I have gathered these." In her mitten, she cupped two small round pills embossed with the letter "B," some white fragments and crumbs. Bayer aspirin! "Send these to your mother for the little ones." By the icicles on her parka, I was certain that Edna had walked ten miles—to two daughters' homes—the length of the village and back to gather the aspirin.

I looked into Edna's clear bright eyes, marveled at her skin crinkled like dried salmon and remembered my visits to her home. Her driftwood and sod hut had no bedroom, no bathroom or running water, much less a medicine cabinet or aspirin. Whenever I arrived at her door, Edna always stood up, offering me her only chair, a rickety one with layers of peeling paint. From under the stove, she brought out a plate of dry pancakes and offered me one, our communion. While we talked or sat in companionable silence, I watched Edna make thread from the dried tendons of caribou. She'd peel a strip of sinew, roll it on the palm of her hand, wet it with her tongue and twist it tightly together with the already worked fiber. Her hands were always busy, sewing, stitching; now, these same hands offered me these pills worth less than a penny.

I thought of my southern California home—five bedrooms, two tiled bathrooms, four medicine cabinets filled with prescriptions and over-the-counter medications. What would my mother think upon receiving the crumbs? Could Mom understand the hugeness of Edna's gift? A small giving, yet the magnitude of Edna's gesture was to become a touchstone for my life.

Tears stung my eyes as I accepted the crumbling aspirin. I could murmur only, "Thank you, Edna."

THE PERFECT LESSON

Lynise Harris

Working as a Peace Corps volunteer in South Africa, I was assigned to schools, one of which was Ikaglaneg. One morning, I arrived at 7:45 a.m. I was there early enough to greet my principal, Ma Hunadi, before morning assembly. When I saw her, she said, "Today is my birthday!"

I had the feeling that she wanted us to do something special for her. I had some gifts my mother sent a few months ago; a day planner, a birthday card, and some wrapping paper and ribbon. I knew this would make a great gift and that she would love the "American" wrapping and style. A surge of energy flowed through my body as I embraced being in charge of something once again. I had been living the ways of the African village for months, and it felt good to be able to show a little "American" culture.

My friend, Victoria, one of the teachers, walked with me the half mile home on the dirt road to get the gift and card. We carefully wrapped the gift and brought the birthday card with us. When we returned, we gathered the teachers secretly to inform them of our gift and to ask them to sign the card. They did not respond. They sat the gift and card down and begin to talk in Northern Sosotho, the language of the village. I sat silently, clueless about what they were discussing. After a few minutes, they got up and went about the day teaching their classes without any response at all. The morning passed.

When school ended that day, we sent the children home. The card was still not signed and the teachers had not told me whether they would participate. They hadn't told me anything. By this point I was frustrated, thinking that these teachers were not wanting to participate in something the "American girl" suggested. I was hurt and angry. I wondered how they could short-change the principal who'd given so much to each of them.

The staff normally gathered in the assistant principal's room (where they'd left the gift) to debrief before going home. Knowing this, I stomped my way to the room to give them a piece of my mind. When I stepped into the room, fuming, I realized they were all there, gathering money to put in the birthday card. Suddenly I dropped my frustration and felt like a fool. They'd sent children to get cookies, punch and formal trays and cups. Minutes later, they each put their financial gift in the card, signed it, gathered the trays, cookies and punch and said, "Khomotso [my South African name which means comfort], it is time!" I smiled and fell in line with them as we marched and danced into the principal's office singing African celebration songs, me mostly humming and listening to them as they harmonized in their beautiful way.

We each gave our blessings and wishes for our principal, Ma Hunadi. Each teacher reminisced about the lessons Ma Hunadi taught, and as each spoke, you would have thought that these speeches had been prepared the night before. We prayed, ate cookies, drank punch and watched as she opened the gift. She cried and said the party was the nicest thing anyone had done for her.

These women blended their traditional African ways with my American ways and the result was spectacular. There was no need to plan, organize, ask permission, or inform me.

I learned an important lesson that day from those women. At times it's better to be a free flowing spirit, believing that whatever happens will be perfect. I don't have to know the outcome of and be in charge of every idea I have. I can let go and allow the idea to manifest beautifully, without stress or friction. I can have faith that whatever is created is perfect.

That afternoon was perfect for the teachers and Ma Hunadi— and oh so perfect for me, a perfect lesson.

AT FACE VALUE

Terry Healey

At the age of twenty, my life had been smooth sailing, seldom interrupted with adversity or difficulty. I was a junior at the University of California at Berkeley and president of my fraternity. I was confident, enjoyed athletics, was doing well in school, and was considered handsome.

But during my junior year, over a period of a couple of weeks, several people asked me what was wrong with my nose. I finally took notice of the bump pushing against my right nostril, but it didn't seem like a big deal. I just assumed it would go away. When it didn't, I made an appointment with a doctor who suggested a biopsy.

It turned out that I had a tumor—a rare fibrosarcoma. Although the bulk of it had been removed during the biopsy, my doctor said I'd need a follow-up surgery to excise any remaining tumor cells. I wasn't alarmed; my assessment of the situation was that I had little to worry about. The procedure proved to be minor. With only a few sutures alongside of my nose and a few more inside my palate, I returned to classes looking like I had been in a fight with *someone*, not *something*.

Six months later, I discovered a new lump rising from the lower portion of my right nostril. Then I began to feel tingling in my cheek. Visits to numerous specialists confirmed that my previously unthreatening tumor had procreated itself into a horrific, life-threatening and potentially disfiguring malignancy. My doctor informed me that I could lose half my nose, half my upper lip and possibly my right eye, but that saving my life was his main concern. I suppose I was too young to contemplate dying, but the realization that I could be disfigured was devastating.

I awoke from the first surgery with a skin graft attached to my face from the skin and fat of my shoulder and chest. Half my nose and upper lip was gone, the muscle and bone from my right cheek had been excised and the shelf of my eye, six teeth, and part of my hard palate had been removed. My doctor's only promise to me was that he would make me "streetable" before I left the hospital. I did not understand at the time that that was his way of preparing me for a life of disfigurement.

When I was released from the hospital, I noticed adults staring at me and children pointing and sometimes laughing at me. I realized that my hospital room had protected me. Outside of it, I was vulnerable and exposed. How was I going to face the world? I cared what other people thought of me. I relished the admiring looks I had received as the "old Terry"' and was petrified of the reaction I'd get as the "new Terry."'

Over the next few months, I encountered many old friends and acquaintances. Their sometimes inadvertently negative reactions and comments left an indelible mark on me. On top of what people were saying, radiation treatments had begun to shrink the tissue on my face, magnifying my deformity. My self-esteem sank lower than I thought possible. I found myself constantly seeking reassurance from people. Did my looks bother them? What did they see? Did they like me? How could they like me?

Five years later and after twenty attempts to reconstruct my face, I was still coping with the insecurity.

When I went in for my last reconstructive procedure, I met a woman who was also being treated at the hospital. We began dating. One day, after listening to me ask her, for the umpteenth time, how she felt about my looks, she ripped into me. The bulk of my problem, she informed me, was not my physical appearance, but my emotional insecurity. Her honesty helped me to realize that surgery would not fix the mental and emotional scars that had become far more disfiguring than the appearance of my face ever had.

I began to examine myself from the inside out. The support of family and friends, prayer, and the realization that my scars were deeper on the inside than the outside all combined to strengthen my spirit and belief in myself. I became a volunteer at The Wellness Community, a cancer support organization that offers hope and support for patients and their families.

Helping others seemed to be the greatest form of therapy. I began to feel better about myself as I realized that I could bring tremendous inspiration and hope to those coping with cancer. Over time, the pain I felt from being an outcast subsided.

Perhaps I will always be an outcast, but it's not pain I feel any more. I am thankful for who I am today—much stronger and wiser than I was before cancer.

We all struggle with insecurities in one form or another. For me it took something devastating—something that would take me to the depths of self-evaluation—to realize that battle scars are what make people interesting; battle scars are what make people wise; battle scars are what make people realize how precious and valuable life really is; battle scars are what prepare people for the inevitable adversity that lies ahead.

SILENT NIGHT

as told to Beth Murphy

⌒

November came, and I had not seen daylight for months. Each day in the concentration camp was the same: down in the darkest places of the earth, breaking stones, building tunnels in the mountains to create an underground airplane factory, where enemy planes could not bomb.

By December the tunnels and the factory were complete. Still I spent long hours under artificial light, never seeing the sky, assembling and dismantling missiles for the German war effort. The dust was so thick that we often couldn't see our hands working. We breathed dirt and sweat.

A man next to me whispered that even God couldn't find us. As Christmas approached, he whispered that Santa Claus could not find us, either.

But Santa Claus did.

This was a small camp, only six hundred or so people—Germans and Austrians, French, Polish, Czechs, and a few Russians. The place had been an old salt mine and warehouses, all surrounded by electrified barbed wire. The cold gnawed at our bones; we lay down on damp planks, and our garments were always sodden from our sweat and the cold.

We were so desperately focused on just getting through the day, on just getting the task at hand complete, that we learned nothing about the person next to us. We could recognize a face, and knew the face's nationality, but there was nothing else left.

Above all else, I remember the hunger. They gave us barely enough to keep us going— the thought of food, the uncertainty of that next meal, made us work even harder. *If we followed the rules, if we did what they said, they would feed us.* Sometimes they fed us, sometimes they did not. Once I met a man who offered a crust of bread in exchange for a discarded cigarette butt: that dry crust—mold on one side—still, all these years later, seems savory and rich and extraordinary.

One day, as Christmas approached, our captors called us out to the common yard in front of the barracks. We dodged one another's gaze.

A staff sergeant stood before us. His shoes glistened in the light. The pleat on his pants was sharp.

Usually the guards' faces were blank: they were robots, just doing their duty. This man, though, seemed to really be look-ing at us, at me—he was really seeing me. With revulsion, per-haps, but pity, too, and compassion.

"It's Christmas," he told us.

We said nothing. What could we say? What did Christmas have to do with the dust, the hunger, and the cold? Christmas should be celebration, and joy, and warmth. Christmas should be filled with light, and we saw only dark.

"It's Christmas," he repeated. "We should celebrate. We should do something to celebrate."

We prisoners glanced at each other, disbelieving.

"Perhaps we could sing?" he went on. "Surely there's a Christmas song we all know?"

And so we sang. Wavering, at first, but we grew heartened as the song went on. We each sang in our own language; we sang badly and out of tune, and it was the most beautiful music in the world: *Stille Nacht* (German) mixed with *Cicha noc* (Polish) and *Nuit de Paix* (French).

We wished the *Silent Night* could go on forever. Suddenly there was kindness, and warmth, and—yes—hope. In the midst of such cruelty, there was hope. Humanity. Such joy, warming us: we sang in our own languages, and when we closed our eyes, we could imagine that we were free—standing in a crowd of carolers like a scene from a Dickens novel: bundled in coats and scarves, awaiting a steaming cup of chocolate.

I remembered the words of my fellow prisoner: that God and Santa Claus could not find us here. We expected God or Santa to perform a miracle—to free us, to strike down our enemies, to make this world better. Right then, standing there singing, I realized that miracles don't happen because God makes them: they happen because *people* make them. We must make miracles happen for ourselves.

The staff sergeant passed around a bottle of alcohol to drink: it was the fuel they used for the missiles. We hadn't been allowed before even to see this liquid. The Germans kept it locked away; they fueled the missiles themselves, not trusting us to touch the stuff. Now here it was—powerful, potent, intoxicating. I drank. The bitterness was sweet.

Next to me a prisoner—a German, I never learned his name—took a swallow and looked up at the sky. I followed his gaze.

The Allies had been making constant air raids, and above us floated the long streams of white vapor from behind the planes. The whole sky was colored with it.

"There," I whispered. "Saint Nicholas, with his long beard. He is protecting us."

And he was.

LOVE THY NEIGHBOR

Kimberly Ripley

Pearlie Mae Maxwell* was elderly and poor. I received her name and biography from a group called The Box Project. It started as a meaningful way to share my family's blessings with someone less fortunate. It turned out to be love.

The Box Project asks donors to provide a monthly box for a person on their list. Their list was composed of elderly folks in rural Mississippi. I received a biography telling me all about Miss Pearlie. She was black. She was in her sixties. Her kidneys were failing and she was on dialysis weekly. She had little to no education and had been widowed for many years. She was a mother and a grandmother. And she had very little in the way of material things. At the suggestion of the program directors, I sent a letter of introduction and awaited a reply. In my letter, I asked her what she most needed or would like to have.

My response from Pearlie Mae was delightful. Her handwriting, although legible, was filled with misspellings and incorrect grammar. Still I deciphered her words and loved their sincerity. She was a humble woman and asked for very little. She considered herself luckier than many of her neighbors.

"I am one of the lucky ones," she wrote. "I have hot water and electricity."

---

*Last name changed for privacy.

I was ashamed to think of the number of times I had complained recently. I complained about our home. I had complained about our yard needing work. And here was this lady feeling blessed for having hot water and electricity!

Her requests were humble, too.

"I'd like some cotton underpants, size ten," she wrote. "And I'd love to have some tin foil."

My first box to Pearlie Mae was filled with kitchen and bathroom things. There were soaps, shampoo, new towels and face cloths. I bought dishtowels for her kitchen, and lots of items she couldn't purchase with her food stamps—paper towels, dish soap, plastic wrap, and several large rolls of good quality tin foil.

Each month brought new surprises—as many for me as for Pearlie. I learned a little more about her with each letter, and was always astonished by her humble requests. Often, she asked for something for one of her daughters, rather than herself.

"Rena needs some shoes," she said.

And she made certain to tell me that the items need not be new.

"We're not proud people," she wrote. "I am happy to have used things that you don't want any more. You don't need to go out and buy new things."

Holidays became even more fun in our family, as my children helped buy the goodies that filled Pearlie Mae's boxes. She loved stuffed animals, so we sent bunnies at Easter, a black cat at Halloween, a turkey at Thanksgiving, and a beautiful calico cat at Christmas time.

When I lost my beloved grandmother in December 1999, I wrote to Pearlie, sharing my sorrows. I was growing more and more fond of this lady, and truly looked forward to her letters. Having misplaced Pearlie's biography sheet after months of sending boxes, I knew she must have a birthday coming up. Hoping I hadn't already missed it, I also asked in this letter when she celebrated her birthday.

My reply came just a few weeks later

"I would love to have a granddaughter like you," she replied, in reference to my loss of my grandmother. "And my birthday is February 20."

I was stunned. That had been my own grandmother's birthday. I believed now, even more, that God had put Pearlie Mae Maxwell and me together for good reason.

I decided to lavish on Pearlie the little pleasures in life my grandmother had loved. I sent letters and cards more often. If I was shopping and saw a pretty blouse and thought, "Gram would have loved that," I'd buy it for Pearlie.

She was delighted when I found size 8 extra-wide shoes.

"All mine fit too snug," she had said.

When the Mississippi wind grew chilly, I found cardigan sweaters that were soft and warm. To make time go by during Pearlie's kidney dialysis appointments, I sent her books on audiocassette and a cassette player.

When Pearlie could no longer stay in her apartment, she moved in with her daughter Dorothy. And although Dorothy and her husband were taking care of her, I wanted to continue sending the boxes. Dorothy had access to a computer, and now we could correspond by e-mail.

"Mama spends a lot of time in bed," Dorothy would write. "Could you send her some night clothes?"

In time Pearlie's material needs became less and less, but it still thrilled me to find little things to send her—things that would have thrilled Gram, like flowers delivered from a florist, a porcelain Easter basket, freshly scented lotions and powders.

As Pearlie's health declined I received updates from Dorothy.

"Mama's taken a turn for the worse," she'd write. "Please pray."

"Let Miss Pearlie know we're praying and we love her," I'd reply.

A few days later I'd rejoice when I received another e-mail.

"She's out of the hospital again."

I could feel God nudging me toward Dorothy. While her needs weren't the same as Pearlie's—I sensed she needed a friend. I sent some uplifting books and some soothing flavored tea. My grandmother had healed everything with prayers and tea.

Finally unable to meet her medical needs, Dorothy regretfully moved her mother into a local nursing home.

"She needs more care than I can give her," she wrote—her message riddled with guilt and sadness.

Messages about Pearlie came weekly, as Dorothy became inundated with nursing home visits.

I sent more flowers.

On a recent night I was surprised to "hear" from Dorothy on a weeknight.

"Mama's not good. Her heart stopped and there's just a machine keeping her alive."

I assured Dorothy once again of our prayers and love. The next day I e-mailed to check on Pearlie's condition.

"Mama left us last night at eleven o'clock," Dorothy wrote. "Her heart stopped three more times and we finally told them they'd done enough."

I never met Pearlie Mae Maxwell, but through the grace of God I knew her and loved her. She was a special part of my life. Her photo hangs today where it has hung for more than three years—on a bulletin board by my desk. Surrounded by pictures of my family, Pearlie looks right at home there. I know with certainty she's right at home with the Lord.

Amen, Indeed

Karen L. Waldman

In my role as a V.A. psychologist, I organized a peer support group for older veterans still struggling with painful military memories. I prayed it would help provide closure on this difficult chapter in their lives.

On the afternoon of the group's seventh meeting, I walked into the brightly lit group room. Sitting in a large circle were nine gray-haired World War II veterans, all of them living libraries with their own unique stories. This assembly of "senior citizens" was an interesting representation of the different branches of the service. On this particular day, several vets started discussing the realism in the movie *Saving Private Ryan*.

"One thing really bothered me," someone hesitantly remarked. All eyes turned toward the voice, waiting for an explanation. D.C., one of two African-American veterans in the group, shared that he only saw white soldiers in the film, even though many African-American men also fought for their country during World War II. He was worried that the younger generations would not recognize the contributions of blacks in American history—not realize that they, too, sacrificed everything, gave their lives for freedom and peace. Across the room, another dark face, somber and deeply wrinkled, nodded in agreement.

A faraway look came into D.C.'s eyes. He began describing what it was like to be a young black soldier during the days of segregation. He recalled completing boot camp and being with hundreds of other young soldiers on a train that was chugging through the South, heading to the East Coast for their deployment overseas. D.C. noted that the men were all tired, hungry, and restless after being cooped up for so long. A stop for dinner was planned en route; a hot meal and change of scenery were eagerly anticipated by all. When the train started slowing down, everyone rose to get off at the upcoming station.

D.C.'s voice suddenly lowered, "Before the doors opened to let anyone out, this young Lieutenant walked into our car, saying he had an announcement to make. He stated that he was very sorry, but that all Negroes would have to stay on the train, assuring us that he would ask the white G.I.s to bring back some food. He explained that people in the area were very prejudiced and that it would be better if we just avoided potential problems by staying on the train. He also told us to lower the blinds on the windows so that no one could see in."

D.C. paused; then asked with a quivering voice, "Can you imagine how hard it was for that poor young lieutenant to have to stand up there and tell all of us colored soldiers that we couldn't get off the train?"

The room fell silent. How many people, I wondered to myself, would be concerned about the lieutenant in that situation? My admiration for D.C. deepened.

Finally, Leroy, the other elderly African-American vet, chimed in, sharing a piece of his own history. It was back in 1944. Wearing his military uniform, this nineteen-year-old soldier was sitting at the back of a bus, anxiously waiting for it to start and take him home for his few days of leave. Other passengers boarded one by one, filling the vehicle to capacity. Finally, the driver got on and headed down the aisle, collecting tickets. When he got to the rear, without even looking at Leroy's ticket, the driver told him that he was on the wrong bus and to get off. Confused, Leroy asked where the bus was headed. When the driver told him, Leroy confirmed that it was his destination, too, displaying his ticket as proof. Again, without even looking at it, the driver repeated that Leroy was on the wrong bus and needed to leave immediately.

"But, sir," the young soldier responded politely, "I just paid six dollars and thirty-five cents for this ticket, so I know it's good. I'm going where you're heading, so this must be the right bus."

The driver responded firmly, "I am in charge, so I can decide whether or not you're on the right bus. Well, I've decided that you are on the wrong one, so get off now."

The other veterans in the room looked at Leroy with immense compassion. This talented jazz musician was a soft-spoken man, an incredibly kind and gentle soul, undoubtedly now just an older version of the young soldier he once was.

He stared straight ahead and spoke once again. "There was this white passenger nearby who overheard the whole conversation. I can still see him. He was a really big man, wearing dark pants and a short-sleeved beige shirt. He stood up in the aisle. I thought he was going to make sure I didn't give the driver any problems and that I got off the bus without making a scene. There was nothing I could say, so I started collecting my gear."

Leroy slowly continued. "But that man, he said to me, 'Stay right there, soldier.' He turned to the bus driver and told him real calm like, 'This young man is serving in the United States Army. He is risking his life for our country. He has a perfectly good ticket, just like the rest of us. He is on the right bus. If he gets off, then the rest of us are going to get off. Aren't we, everybody?' By then, everyone had been looking at us and listening to what was going on. At first I felt a little scared and even a little ashamed. No one moved or said a word. Then that man in the dark pants started gathering up his belongings and repeated to all the other passengers, 'If this soldier has to get off the bus, then the rest of us are going to get off, too. Aren't we?'

"Well, it was like a miracle. One by one, every single person on that crowded bus started picking up their things and standing, ready to walk off at a moment's notice. They all waited for the bus driver's response. Well, do you know that man didn't say another word? He just glared at me, grabbed the ticket out of my hand, walked back down the aisle, and got into the driver's seat. All those other people just looked at me and smiled. There was no way that I could repay them. But mostly, I'll never forget that man in the dark pants who stood up for me."

Leroy's eyes were not the only ones filled with tears. He slowly scanned the circle of aging men and commented softly, "I can't believe that I'm in this room today, talking like this with so many other veterans, sitting here next to each other. Once we were separated from one another—couldn't eat together, couldn't bunk together, couldn't even serve in the same units. I don't see the color of anyone's skin in this room. All I see are men like me, just other American veterans who all served our country, who have the same color of blood. I love you, my brothers."

Leroy spontaneously reached out his right hand and took the hand of the man sitting next to him. John instantly did the same, and the gesture continued all around the room with Charles, Sam, D.C., Andy, George, Bill, and Ron.

A peaceful silence filled the room, and it somehow seemed even more brilliantly lit than before. The men quietly exchanged smiles, sharing an unspoken bond, ignoring the emotional intensity and potential awkwardness of the moment. Finally, D.C. raised both arms high in the air, his strong dark hands still holding those of the men sitting next to him. He joyfully bellowed, "Amen!"

As if rehearsed, the others instantly raised their arms, too, simultaneously repeating, "Amen!" They broke into laughter, then stood and hugged one another.

Amen, indeed, I silently echoed. Some prayers are answered before our very eyes.

WHAT I LEARNED FROM CONNIE

Kathie Weir

In 1987, I was blessed with two miracles: my first child, Sierra, and a loving childcare expert, Connie. They didn't arrive together. After a week or two with my baby bundle of nonstop demands, I realized my new child had neglected to read the fine print in my parenting books. She had no intention of sleeping through the night or at any time. I now faced the new major issue of my life: what to do with baby when I cleaned, shopped, cooked, had free time, and eventually returned to work?

No family members were available to help. I sought childcare among neighbors, friends, and parenting co-ops, but soon learned two things: I had a "high needs" baby and caregivers preferred the "sleeping infant" model.

Connie, the first woman to answer my newspaper ad, had a round face and a long black braid. At thirty-two, she looked eighteen. Smiling, she stepped inside and opened her arms.

"Give me the baby!" she said invitingly. Amazingly, my five-month-old reached back. Sierra played with Connie's braid as Connie bounced and cuddled her. She had clearly found someone who met her standards.

Connie's first trip to the nearby park lasted over two hours. New mom jitters sent me rushing to the park with visions of children being sold to the highest bidder. How foolish I felt when I saw Connie sitting quietly in the shade, Sierra asleep on her lap.

As months passed, I learned more from Connie about nurturing and patience than I had gleaned from my life experience or parenting books. Connie's parents had seventeen children. Of the fourteen who survived, only Connie was childless. Yet, her intuitive mothering worked like a tranquilizer on my overactive baby.

Many question the wisdom of hiring non-English-speakers for childcare. Although Connie was part time and I was nearby, friends warned that my children wouldn't recognize me or would develop poor language skills. Her natural intelligence led her to learn almost flawless English. She preferred English, though now I regret that she didn't teach my children Spanish.

When I met Connie and her husband, Blas, in 1987, they had recently been granted amnesty after sixteen years in the United States. They earned a decent living, but lived in a cramped apartment in a bad area, fearful of moving up, then suffering a job loss. They never took their good fortune for granted.

Connie and Blas were raised in a rural area near Zacatecas, Mexico. As teens, they followed relatives to the U.S. Having grown up in rural poverty in the northeast, I thought I understood their background. Then one day, I peeled an apple for Sierra. When she asked for more, Connie seemed to take forever to peel another. I wondered why. Later, I saw two adjacent piles of peelings. Mine were close to a quarter inch thick. Connie's peelings were paper-thin, looking almost as if she'd scraped them off with her fingernail. Her memory of poverty was deeply engrained, translating to a reverence for all food, even tiny bits of apple on the inside of a peeling. Clearly, I had forgotten the truths of poverty. I understood so much about her and about myself that day.

Working an erratic at-home schedule, I was isolated, neither a full-time professional nor a "stay-at-home mom." Connie became my anchor and confidante. She absorbed my "new-mother" confusion and the frequent chaos of our household. At the root of it all was her essential female role training: *give, give, give; don't question.* I could never have paid Connie enough for what she gave us.

When I was eight months pregnant with my son, she asked if she could feel him move. Since her mother had home-birthed her children, I had assumed that Connie had seen many births. In fact, she said she would go to bed at night and wake up to find her mother with a new baby. Breastfeeding was unknown to her; her relatives had used formula. Another misconception on my part.

When Brett was born, Connie proved equally competent at watching two children. She gave picturesque updates of the kids' words and actions while they were with her. Not just a caretaker; she was a loving aunt, an adoring grandmother, a best friend, and a surrogate mother, all in one. Even if I didn't have work, I often asked her to join me and the kids for a shopping trip or day at the park.

Connie's expertise with children was matched by Blas's expertise with nature. He planted a garden and we shared his strawberries, tomatoes, green chili, and corn. When an unethical employer cheated him, I intervened; he was reimbursed. When I was sick or on a difficult deadline, Connie extended her hours.

When she told us Blas had decided to return to Mexico, and that she'd be leaving, too, we were heartbroken. For years, Blas had cleaned oil tanks in the harbor. His health suffered. He had carefully saved and invested in twenty acres of Mexican land, a tractor, and livestock. At last, he had saved enough to return and build his house.

Connie gave two months' notice. We both cried every day until she left. I found it confusing that the very traits and behaviors that I had spent decades pushing to the background were the qualities that I cherished in Connie. Connie didn't want to leave. I urged her to stay with us, at least until Blas finished their house.

"He is my husband. I go with him where he goes," she said. Blas didn't ask her opinion. My feminist side didn't approve of her unquestioning loyalty. As a woman, I admired and in some ways envied Connie's ability to follow his path.

For years after they moved, Connie visited for two to four weeks at a time. Our house would be filled with the smell of roasting green chilies. My children followed her around as she entertained everyone with stories of her new ranch life. We haunted thrift stores for clothes that she could take back to relatives.

Connie and Blas have lived in Mexico for over ten years now. They aren't rich, but they survive. Two-and-a-half years ago, at age 46, Connie gave birth to a son, an unexpected blessing. She tried to visit us when her baby was six months old, but found that she couldn't bring him across the border because he was born in Mexico and she still has a green card.

We last saw her when we drove to Tijuana to spend a few hours with her in the noisy town square, all of us feeling like refugees. She applied for the paperwork to bring her son across the border, but it could take years for approval. We hugged good-bye, not knowing when we would meet again.

I write to Connie, but gifts tend to "get lost" in Mexico. Our family often reminisces about Connie and Blas. They live three miles from the nearest phone, but she tries to call on our birth-days. When one of my children hears her voice, his or her eyes light up; a mixture of yearning and delight enters the voice. How ironic that the very thing that brought Connie and I together, children, now keeps us apart.

I miss Connie as one would miss a sister, a mentor, and a best friend. Our bond was formed in the most mundane of circum-stances, but carried with it a profound discovery. By meeting each other's needs, we accessed a deeper and larger culture of mothers, children, and families, a culture that transcends bor-ders and offers safe harbor to all.

FEELING THE LOVE TOGETHER

Stevie Wonder

My defining moment was discovering God's love and our own human purpose: striving to value the other guy as much as we value ourselves. To me, Dr. Martin Luther King exemplified that higher purpose. I only met him once, but that's what he represented to me. Nelson Mandela represents it as well, along with all the other leaders and ordinary people who step beyond themselves and value the importance of others.

I remember once when I was a little boy living in Detroit, maybe eight or nine years old, I was listening to the radio and I heard about some kids who died in a fire. The parents had left the children alone, and the children were playing with matches. The house caught on fire, and the children burned with it. I remember being so upset when I heard that this happened just a few blocks from where I lived on Twenty-fourth Street— hearing about it just hurt my heart. So I went over and touched the house. That was all—I just touched the house. I don't know if I had a more vivid imagination, being blind and not really able to see it, if maybe that made it all clearer to my heart. But my heart went out for those kids. And even though it hurt so much, I felt that I was in touch with the love that God had told us about, the love that finds a way to care about everyone, even the people we don't know, even the people we're not related to. Because in the end, we all are related. We may not all be the same, and that's O.K. But the most important part of us is the same.

So I believe the most important thing we can do is to have compassion for each other. Our common goal has got to be caring. What if we took the pain we might feel if we lost the most important person in our life, and then felt that pain for other people? People who are not related to us—but who *are* related in that they are part of our community, part of our universe. If we can feel for those other people the way we'd feel for ourselves, then we've achieved our highest purpose.

That's our biggest challenge, and we don't always succeed. We may only be works in progress. But let's at least *be* works in progress! Let's try to achieve that caring.

My own personal purpose, I think, is to do the very best I can, to use the gift God has given me, to communicate what I've learned through the lyrics and music that I write.

I believe music helps create that common thread, tying us all together.

Sometimes people will talk to me about one of my songs. They'll say, "'I Just Called To Say I Love You,' you know, I sing that to my kids every day," or "I sing it to my wife every day before I go to work," or "My husband used to sing it to me, and now he's gone, but when I listen to that song, it's like he's here." Music allows us to get caught up in that place where we can all share, we can all care for each other.

Sometimes I'll write a song for a specific purpose. I wrote "Happy Birthday" because there was a big struggle about whether or not we'd get a national holiday to celebrate Martin Luther King's birthday. Mrs. Coretta Scott King was leading the lobbying efforts to petition Congress, and thousands of people were organizing and fighting to make this a reality. But for a while it didn't look good. Some people thought of the holiday as just for Black people, and they didn't see why a national holiday should honor one special group. Some folks thought that adding a new national holiday would be too expensive, that businesses couldn't afford to pay people for a day when they weren't working. And some people probably didn't like Dr. King's legacy in the first place, though they didn't necessarily come right out and say so.

So even though there was a tremendous movement pushing for this new holiday, there were plenty of discouraging times. I know I got discouraged, and so did the folks I worked with. So finally, I just said, "Listen, we're going to get a holiday." I just felt it in my mind. And the moment I said it, I knew it would be a reality—and I was determined to do whatever I had to do to help make it a reality. So I wrote that song.

I would like to think that what my song did for the movement was to help make it clear why *everybody* had a stake in Martin Luther King Day–not just Black folks, but everybody who believed in what Dr. King stood for. So here's some of what I wrote:

> You know it doesn't make much sense
> There ought to be a law against
> Anyone who takes offense
> At a day in your celebration . . .

> * * *

> Why has there never been a holiday
> Where peace is celebrated
> all throughout the world

The time is overdue
For people like me and you
Who know the way to truth
Is love and unity to all God's children . . .

So let us all begin
We know that love can win
Let it out don't hold it in
Sing it loud as you can

Happy birthday to you
Happy birthday to you
Happy birthday

We know the key to unify all people
Is in the dream that you had so long ago
That lives in all of the hearts of people
That believe in unity
We'll make the dream become a reality
I know we will because our hearts tell us so

After I finished the song, we started our summer tour. Bob Marley was supposed to come with us, but he got sick, so we had Gil Scott-Heron instead. And from the moment we started singing "Happy Birthday" and talking about the holiday, everyone in the audience was saying things like, "Yes. We're here. And this is going to happen." And you could just feel the energy every time we sang that song, moving between us and the audience. And then the audience brought that energy with them out into the lobby, where they signed a petition for the holiday, and then they brought it with them into the street, and into their homes, and to all the other places that they went. Something about that song just tapped into the power of the good, the power of the positive, the power of us all together.

And then we won. Finally, the bill was going to be signed. Just about that time, we were giving a concert at the Capitol Theatre in Washington, D.C. That was a really magical moment. Everyone in the audience was singing with us, thousands of voices all singing "Happy Birthday" to Dr. King. Everyone was overjoyed, because this was a victory in the making for everyone, and the energy just kept getting higher and higher and higher. And to me, that's what it's all about—all of us trying our very best to make a difference, and then feeling the love together.

After the Rain

Laura Stamps

What if one morning,
when the coverlet of rain recedes
and the sun offers its fiery feathers
on the white altar of a gardenia,
you were to discover that you are not
what you seem to be?
What if you were to believe
deep in your heart that you are a spirit,
divinely dressed in a cloak of humanity,
here on earth for seventy
or eighty years to bless everyone
you meet with heavenly love?
What if this were your only intention,
simple and true?
O how the meadowlark, cardinal,
and field sparrow would play
the blue lute of the sky.
O how your life would change.

ABOUT THE CONTRIBUTORS

Muhammad Ali: Muhammad Ali became world heavyweight champion in 1964. Stripped of his title for refusing to fight in the Vietnam War, Ali went on to win the title two more times, becoming the first three-time heavyweight champion in boxing history. He is the founder of the Muhammad Ali Center in Louisville, Kentucky (www.alicenter.org), dedicated to preserving Ali's legacy of supporting peace, social justice, and respect for all humans.

Maya Angelou: Dr. Maya Angelou is a remarkable Renaissance woman who is hailed as one of the great voices of contemporary literature. As a poet, educator, historian, bestselling author, actress, playwright, civil rights activist, producer and director, she continues to travel the world, spreading her legendary wisdom. Within the rhythm of her poetry and elegance of her prose lies Angelou's unique power to help readers of every orientation span the lines of race. For more information, see www.mayaangelou.com.

Rev. Michael Beckwith: Michael Beckwith, D.D., is the founder and spiritual director of Agape International Spiritual Center in Culver City, California, one of the world's most rapidly growing multiracial, multicultural spiritual communities in the New Thought/Ancient Wisdom tradition of spirituality. He is the author of *40 Day Mind Fast Soul Feast* and *A Manifesto of Peace.*

Elizabeth L. Blair: Elizabeth Blair resides in Arizona with her husband Jeff. She works as a freelance writer and a flight attendant. Currently, she is working on her first book, tales of her humorous journeys in the airline industry.

Arthur Bowler: Arthur Bowler, a Massachusetts native who now lives in Switzerland, is a writer, speaker, and minister in English and in German. A graduate of Harvard Divinity School, Arthur Bowler has appeared in the *Chicken Soup for the Soul* series and in a bestseller published in Switzerland.

Caroline Castle Hicks: Caroline Castle Hicks is a former English teacher who is now a freelance writer, poet, and frequent public radio commentator. Her work appears in two editions of the *Chicken Soup for the Soul* series as well as numerous other publications. She lives in a suburb of Charlotte, North Carolina, with her husband and their two children.

Margaret Cho: Margaret Cho is a comedian and writer. She has been honored by organizations including GLAAD, AWRT, LLDEF, NGLTF, AALDEF, and NOW for "making a significant difference in promoting equal rights for all, regardless of race, sexual orientation, or gender identity." For more information on Margaret, please visit www.margaretcho.com

Shae Cooke: Shae Cooke, a Canadian inspirational writer, contributing author, mother, and former foster child, shares her heart, humor, daily foibles, and God's message of hope internationally, in print and online.

Cheryl Costello-Forshey: Cheryl Costello-Forshey is a poet and short story writer. Her work has been published in several of the *Chicken Soup for the Soul* books, *No Body's Perfect, Stories for a Faithful Heart, Stories for a Teen's Heart, Stories for a Teen's Heart 2, A Pleasant Place,* and *Serenity for a Woman's Heart.*

Megan Katherine Dahle: Megan Dahle attends high school in Fort Worth, Texas. Through her observation of the self among others (and the world), she wrote the poem "One."

Andrew Dan-Jumbo: Andrew Dan-Jumbo has lived in the United States for ten years, working as a carpenter with his brother in a firm they cofounded, Eurotek, a construction company based in Buffalo, New York. He has recently become a household name as the featured carpenter of the hit series, *While You Were Out*, and was named as one of *People* magazine's fifty most beautiful people.

Linda Darby Hughes: Linda Darby Hughes is a freelance writer in Douglasville, Georgia. She and her husband, Johnnie, were foster parents for sixteen years, and kept over one hundred children in need before adopting a son, Robert, in 1996. Her work has appeared in numerous publications, including *The Hometown Advantage, Mature Living Magazine*, and *The Atlanta Journal and Constitutio*n.

Diane Haldane-Doerr: Diane Haldane-Doerr lives in Charlotte, North Carolina, with her husband Rob and daughter Ryan. She is proud to belong to a multicultural family—by chance and chosen.

Dr. Randall Hardy: Dr. Randall Hardy is a retired chiropractor/naturopath and the former health director of a major destination health resort. He is now working as a weight management and lifestyle coach and as a health and self-development writer and lecturer. Randall is a member of the National Speakers Association and the author or coauthor of two books. He is married to Marian.

Lynise Harris: Lynise Harris is a personal life coach and the first African American to be certified by the Life on Purpose Institute. She works with professionals who are launching their own business, are in career transition, or are simply looking for more out of life. She lives in San Antonio, Texas. You can contact her at http://www.livelyliving.net.

Terry Healy: Terry Healey is a motivational speaker and the author of *At Face Value: My Struggle with a Disfiguring Cancer*. He has been published in *Psychology Today*, *The San Francisco Chronicle*, and *Coping Magazine*. For more information about his speaking and his book, please visit his website http://www.at-face-value.com.

Kim Huong Marker: Kim Huong Marker emigrated to the United States from Vietnam in 1973. She lives with her husband in western Maryland. Kim received her social work degree in 2001. She is the director for a transitional housing program that provides support to homeless families.

Eric Anthony Ivory: Eric Anthony Ivory was born and grew up in Oakland, California, to parents whose ancestry includes African, American Indian, and European. He is currently a professor at Modesto Junior College in Modesto, California.

Shirley Jackson-Avery: Shirley Jackson-Avery resides in Odenton, Maryland, with her husband and two children. Currently, she is a guidance counselor with Anne Arundel County Public Schools and writes short stories and poems in her free time.

Paul Karrer: Paul Karrer has published five stories in the *Chicken Soup* series. He can be heard each month reading his short stories on KUSP 88.9 FM, Santa Cruz, California. He taught in Korea, England, California, American Samoa, and was a Peace Corps instructor in Western Samoa.

Robert F. Kennedy, Jr.: Robert Francis Kennedy Jr. is the third of eleven children born to Robert Francis Kennedy and Ethel Kennedy. He is the president of the Waterkeepers Alliance and a prosecuting attorney for the Riverkeepers.

Sarah Kay Kessler: Sarah Kay Kessler is studying music performance on flute and journalism at Ithaca College, in New York state, where she received a full-tuition scholarship based on her diversity awareness and her community service and sense of community. She lives in Fulton, New York.

Steven Manchester: The father of two sons, Steven works as a technical writer for State Street Bank. As a freelance writer, he has published more than eighty articles, both local and abroad. His work has been showcased in such national literary journals as *Taproot Literary Review, American Poetry Review* and *Fresh! Literary Magazine*. He currently publishes monthly installments of fiction with *Titan Magazine* and *Skyline Literary Magazine*, and has also contributed essays, poetry, and short fiction to various internet publications.

Marie McBride: Since retiring as administrative director for a nonprofit agency for prevention and treatment of child abuse, Marie McBride has devoted herself to writing. She lives in Charlotte, North Carolina, and has been married for forty years. She has two children and two grandsons and is a former teacher and parenting instructor.

Beth Murphy is a documentary producer and director, author and university professor. This story is an excerpt from *The Unlikely Santa*, Beth's upcoming documentary featuring Holocaust survivor John Torunski. As the founder and president of Principle Pictures, Inc., Beth thanks her father, Howard Brundage, for introducing her to John's inspiring story and wisdom.

Shinan Naom Barclay: Shinan Naom Barclay is an award-winning speaker, storyteller, and performance artist. Her writing appears in the anthologies *Heavenly Helpings, Scent of Cedars*, and *Chicken Soup for Woman's Soul II*. She is the coauthor of *Flowering Woman, Moontime for Kory* (a girl's rite of passage into womanhood), and *The Sedona Vortex Experience*. Contact her at www.shinanagans.com.

James Gerard Noel: James Noel was born in England. He has been living in the United States for the past four years and is an aspiring writer.

Adoralida (Dora) Padilla: Dora is a worker's compensation judge for the state of California. She resides in her native city of San Jose with her husband John and their son Jonathan.

Freddie Ravel: In his innovative concert and speaking presentation, Tune Up to Success™ (www.TuneUptoSuccess.com), number one multiplatinum recording artist, Freddie Ravel demonstrates that music is the perfect metaphor and solution to overcoming communication obstacles in the dynamics of business.

Sharon Redhawk Love, Ph.D.: Dr. Sharon Redhawk Love is a Native American woman of the Blackfoot and Eastern Cherokee nations. She is an educator, counselor, writer, and researcher. Her academic background includes criminology, minority/ethnic groups, sociology, and women's studies. Her recent research has focused on women and crime. Her personal web page is http://www.personal.psu.edu/faculty/s/r/srl11/.

Rabbi Jack Reimer: Rabbi Jack Reimer is a distinguished writer and editor whose prayers appear in the prayerbooks of the Conservative and Reform movements in the United States and abroad. He is the coeditor of *So That Your Values Live On, A Treasury of Ethical Wills*, published by Jewish Lights.

Beatrice M. Rembert: Beatrice M. Rembert, born in Miami, Florida, served six years active duty service in the U.S. Army and recently obtained a B.A. in psychology from St. Martin's College in Lacey, Washington. Her family includes her children, Daquan, Maya, and DeMarquis, and husband Darrin Rembert.

Kim Ripley: Kimberly Ripley is a freelance writer and published author from Portsmouth, New Hampshire. She travels frequently, facilitating her "Freelancing Later in Life" writing workshop. Her family includes her husband Roland, children Scott, Judy, Jim, Elizabeth, and Jonathan. She is also a home-schooler and frequently writes on the topic.

LaVonne Schoneman: LaVonne Schoneman is a writer living in Seattle, Washington. Her published works include the How to Cope book series, articles, short stories, screenplays, fiction, novels, and poetry appearing nationally and internationally. She is also a multilingual actress, artist, teacher, wife, mother, and grandmother who has traveled extensively and lived in Mexico.

Bernie Siegel, M.D.: Dr. Siegel, who prefers to be called Bernie, not Dr. Siegel, was born in Brooklyn, New York. In 1978 he originated Exceptional Cancer Patients (www.ecap-online.org). Bernie and his wife and coworker Bobbie live in New Haven, Connecticut. Bernie and Bobbie have coauthored their children, books, and articles. In 1986 his first book, *Love, Medicine & Miracles*, was published. This event redirected his life. In 1989 *Peace, Love & Healing* was published, and his latest books are *Prescriptions for Living*, *Help Me To Heal: All to Empower People*, and *Patients in the Art Of Healing*.

Amy Skirvin: As a sophomore in high school, Amy Maddox wrote "Underneath We Are All The Same." She is now Amy Skirvin and still a small-town girl. She lives in Indiana with her husband, Steve.

Laura Stamps: Laura Stamps is the author of more than twenty books of poetry and prose. Hundreds of her poems, short stories, and poetry book reviews have appeared in literary journals, magazines, and anthologies. Her poetry books are archived by the University Libraries at SUNY, Buffalo, New York. Currently she is at work on a novel.

Mattie J. T. Stepanek: Matthew J.T. Stepanek, best known as "Mattie," has been writing poetry and short stories since age three. His books of poetry are titled *Heartsongs, Journey Through Heartsongs, Hope Through Heartsongs*, and *Celebrate Through Heartsongs*. Mattie is a frequent public speaker, who has appeared on *Oprah, Good Morning America*, and *Larry King* and has had his poetry published in newspapers and magazines nationwide. Mattie serves as the National Goodwill Ambassador for the Muscular Dystrophy Association (www.mdausa.org).

Deborah C. Thomas: Deborah C. Thomas lived in Asia from 1976 to 1991 while employed as a social worker. She is currently a youth program director for several faith-based community churches, and her curriculum focuses on teaching children the value of thinking, speaking, and acting peacefully.

Beverly Tribuiani-Montez: Beverly Tribuiani-Montez is a wife and the mother of two little girls, Jessica and Sophie. She has been writing all her life, as a way of processing life and for the opportunity to touch people in a familiar voice

Karen L. Waldman: Karen L.Waldman, Ph.D., is a psychologist who works with a diverse group of veterans. She also enjoys writing, learning, acting, nature, music, traveling with her husband Ken, and "playing" with their wonderful friends, relatives, children, and grandchildren.

Michele Wallace Campanelli: Michele Wallace Campanelli is a nationally renowned, bestselling author. She is the author of over twenty-two anthologized short stories and has penned several novels, including *Keeper of the Shroud* and *Margarita* published by Americana Books. She was born on the Space Coast of Florida, where she resides with her husband, Louis V. Campanelli III. To contact Michele, go to www.michelecampanelli.com.

Jimmi Ware: A writer for over twenty years, Jimmi Ware loves poetry and frequently performs his works. He has produced two cable access programs, one of which received an award from the Alliance for Community Media in Washington, D.C. Ware is involved in his community and is a foster parent.

Abby Warmuth: Abby Warmuth was raised in suburban Detroit and graduated from the University of Michigan with a major in English. After spending nine years in business, she is now a writer. She currently lives in Fort Mill, South Carolina, with her husband, Jorg.

Julie Wassom Melton: Julie Wassom Melton is a professional speaker, author, and consultant. In addition to being the mother in a multicultural family, Julie is an advocate for parents of children with special needs. She is the author of *A Seed of Hope—The Survival Guide for Parents of Children with Special Needs*. You can contact her at www.juliewassom.com

Kathie Weir: Kathie Weir is the author of *A Parent's Guide to Los Angeles* and *A Parent's Guide to School Projects*. Her short stories have been featured in Sally Shore's New Short Fiction series, and her poems, essays, and articles have appeared in various journals and books. She and her two teenage children live in the Los Angeles area.

Larraine R. White: Larraine White ran a day care program in her home for twelve years. During that time, she home-schooled her four children through junior high. At present, she owns a long-distance consulting business, TeleConsulting Services. She has been published in *F.A.C.E. Facts* (Families Adopting Children Everywhere) and *True Love*.

Josie Willis: Josie Willis's voice has been heard in *Chicken Soup for the Writer's Soul, Florida Gardening, Mike Shayne Mys-*

tery, and *Highlight for Children* magazines and in numerous inspirational poetry books published by Blue Mountain Arts. She is currently working on a book about child abuse.

Stevie Wonder: Singer, composer, musician, and producer, Stevie Wonder has been making music for almost four decades. Blind since birth, he has been performing since childhood. Stevie has written many songs on peace, justice, and the common humanity that the world shares. He has been the recipient of numerous awards, including twenty-two Grammys, along with an Oscar for "I Just Called to Say I Love You."

ACKNOWLEDGMENTS

Open My Eyes, Open My Soul has been a divinely guided project from the start. The manuscript took less than one year, approximately ten months, to complete. We believe that the hand of our Creator has been here every step of the way to ensure that the right people and the right doors were opened for us to get this message into the hands of our readers. So first we must thank God for the blessings brought into our lives by giving us the vision, the passion, and the means to be the instruments for which this message has come through.

Of course a project like this does not come to fruition without the support of many individuals who share a passion for the mission we wish to accomplish. There are so many people who have lent a hand in one way or another, and we will do our best to give honor to all of you, but if we leave someone out on paper, know that you are unconditionally loved and never forgotten in our hearts.

First of all, a special thank you to Mark Victor Hansen and Jack Canfield, who paved the way for later anthologies with their famous *Chicken Soup for the Soul*. Mark, you have been an incredible mentor to Elodia. Without Mark's encouragement and support of those of us who wished to be published, this project might never have been attempted.

A special thank you to Yolanda's mother, Mrs. Coretta Scott King, for her beautiful foreword to our book. It brought tears to the eyes of both of us when reading it for the first time. To

Elodia's parents and to her children, Danae, Devaun, Dionne, and Derek, who have been understanding when their mother has had to make sacrifices with them. To both of our families and friends, who offered their prayers and shared words of encouragement, supporting our project every step of the way. We are blessed to have far too many of you to name personally, but you know who you are.

We would not have this special collection of stories without the contributions from those of you around the world who wrote stories and poems or who graciously granted us interviews and gave us approval to use your quotations, and to your assistants, who helped facilitate the process. We are honored to have received such wonderful contributions for our project. There are several hundred selections that are beautiful and that we loved, but could not find room for in this book. We appreciate all of the efforts our contributors have made, regardless of whether they are included in this book. We feel most richly blessed to have been showered with so much wonderful material from which we could choose. We also want to thank those who helped us spread the word that we were looking for stories. They include Susan Levin, Lottie Robins, Maureen Ryan Griffin, Caroline Hicks, Brad Swift, and Kimberly Ripley. Thanks also to our previously unpublished authors who participated in the contest and got hundreds of family members and friends to vote on our website: James Noel, Kim Huong-Marker, Adoralida Padilla, Jimmi Ware, and our winner, Abby Warmuth, for her story "Danny."

Our final selections came from the help of a dedicated team of people, who understood our mission and spent countless hours reading and rating our material: Al Smith, Eric Ivory, Renee Kee, Gail Clark, Ann Kline, Judge Dora Lopez, Michelle

Murphy, Rema Caspillo, Tanya White, Wanda Marie, and Ron Lapointe. A special thank you to Pamela Crittenden, for helping assemble our team of readers at Modesto Junior College in California, otherwise known as MJC. Also, for Pamela's countless hours editing, driving, traveling, or showing up with Starbucks coffees in the late hours of the night when needed, and to her family, Michael, Omari, and Naya, for allowing us to take their wife and mother away from their family to help with this project.

To Quentin and Lisa Anderson, for their loving support and a place to stay and work while researching this project. To Shawna and Barry Richardson, for their help setting up the office and being there to fix whatever needed fixing. To Joanne Cowdrey, for transportation. To Carolyn Hagen, who spent hours on the phone counseling and even flew out from Texas to make sure Elodia got out and took a break. To Michael Chambers, for holding off on the roof. To Jorden Boom, for his web site help, and to Julie Sanchez, for her computer help. To Julie Wassom Melton and Ashley Tyler, for their help in brainstorming for a book title, and to the many others who voted online. To Wanda Marie, for her invaluable suggestions and support from the very beginning. To Debbie and Heinrich Wolski, for their help with initial artwork possibilities. To Wendi Huntley, for legal advice. To Dee Foderingham, for makeup, to Jon Michael Terry, for photography, and to Jennifer Bayse Sanders, for guidance and a lead to our wonderful literary agent, Jeffrey Kleinman, who arrived just in the nick of time. To Nancy Hancock and Meg Leder at McGraw-Hill, for all of their editing expertise, and the rest of the McGraw-Hill team for their enthusiasm and hard work: Philip Ruppel, Lynda Luppino, Lizz Aviles, Eileen Lamadore, Lydia Rinaldi, Scott Kurtz, Maureen

Harper, and Tom Lau. To the energetic Rachel Kranz, for her help and writing expertise.

To all of our wonderful friends, who spent time reading the advance copies of our manuscript and who gave us their heartfelt words in the form of an endorsement.

Finally, to you, the reader, for picking up our book and continuing to pass along the torch by sharing it with others.

About Yolanda King

Yolanda King is an internationally recognized motivational speaker and actor. Born in Montgomery, Alabama, she is the first child of Dr. Martin Luther King, Jr., and Coretta Scott King. Yolanda has been in the midst of the quest for human rights and peace all of her life. She has performed or lectured in forty-nine of the fifty American states as well as in Europe, Africa, and Asia for educational, business, religious, and civic organizations. Sharing her message of the importance of embracing our common humanity, Yolanda has sounded the call from the halls of the United Nations to venues in Moscow and Munich. Yolanda King has been acclaimed for her ability to inspire people to reach higher ground, to motivate people to move forward, and to empower people to make a difference.

As a seasoned and respected actor, many of Ms. King's stage, television, and film credits reflect her commitment to personal and social change and include portrayals of Rosa Parks in the NBC-TV movie *King*, Dr. Betty Shabazz in the film *Death of a Prophet* with Morgan Freeman, and Medgar Evers' daughter, Reena, in *Ghosts of Mississippi*. Focusing on the highlights of the Civil Rights Movement, Yolanda King's most recent theatrical production, *Achieving the Dream*, in which she portrays several characters, is a product of her unique relationship with her father and her deep insight into this pivotal time in our history.

Ms. King has been honored with numerous presentations, awards, and citations by organizations around the country, and she has been named one of the Outstanding Young Women of America.

About Elodia Tate

Elodia Tate grew up in a culturally diverse neighborhood in San Jose, California. Although Elodia's father is Caucasian and Native American, her mother is a blend of Spanish, Native American, and Mexican descent.

Elodia has worked in the mortgage industry and has written for newsletters specializing in the mortgage arena for homeowners and contributed to local newspapers. In the early 1990s, Elodia discovered that she had lupus. In 1995 she was able put the illness in remission by taking a natural approach to managing her health. That event sparked an eagerness to learn and share all she could in the natural health industry. After studying, she spent time speaking to small groups and large audiences about her experience with taking a natural approach to health. She has written articles for several online magazines and continues to speak about her experiences.

Elodia's four children have an ethnicity that is a blend of African American and her own Hispanic, Caucasian, and Native American descent. Living with them as a multicultural family and seeing firsthand the issues of diversity are what brought about her urge to bring awareness and enlightenment so that we may walk a more peaceful path on this planet.

ABOUT OUR WORK

Our Vision: We envision a world where there is peace and unity among all people, where brotherhood and sisterhood become a reality and the Dream is no longer a dream.

Our Mission: Our mission is to use *Open My Eyes, Open My Soul* as the first of many books and other offerings that provide insight, wisdom, and inspiration by opening the eyes and touching the souls of individuals all over the world so that we all may see differently and come to feel and know our common unity.

Our Goal: Our goal is twofold. First our goal is to get this book and similar offerings into the hands of men, women, and children of every race, religion, and culture all around the globe to start the process of opening everyone's eyes (particularly our children's) and spreading the message about our common unity. The second part of our goal is to partner with specific nonprofit organizations on a similar mission of spreading peace and nonviolence by contributing part of the proceeds from this book to help advance their mission. For this first book we have joined in partnership with The Martin Luther King Junior Center for Nonviolent Social Change and the Teaching Tolerance Program in recognition and support of their ongoing work toward global peace.

How You Can Help: You, each individual and every organization, can help us to fulfill our mission and to realize the vision of a better world by sharing this first book with your family and friends, by giving books as gifts to those in need of encouragement. Teachers can make this book available to their students, corporations can offer books to their associates, churches can have books available for their congregation. We know you will find creative ways to help in the promotion of peace and unity.

Contact Us: If you have a story or poem that resonates with our mission that you would like to share in our future book projects, please visit our website at www.openmyeyesopenmysoul.com to submit your work or receive more information. You may also submit work by regular mail to:

Let's Dream – Soul Project
Post Office Box 578325
Modesto, CA 95357

To contact Yolanda King for speaking engagements, please call her executive coordinator at 323-295-4144 or visit www.Yolanda-King.com.

To contact Elodia Tate for speaking engagements, please contact her at 209-238-9938 or visit www.elodiatate.com.

A portion of our proceeds from the sale of *Open My Eyes, Open My Soul* will be donated to the following organizations:

The King Center
449 Auburn Ave. NE
Atlanta, GA 30312
(404) 526-8900
www.thekingcenter.org

Established in 1968 by Coretta Scott King, The King Center is the official living memorial dedicated to the advancement of the legacy of Dr. Martin Luther King, Jr., leader of America's greatest nonviolent movement for justice, equality, and peace.

and

Teaching Tolerance
c/o The Southern Poverty Law Center
400 Washington Ave.
Montgomery, AL 35104
(334) 956-8200
www.tolerance.org

Tolerance.org is an online destination for people interested in dismantling bigotry and hate in communities that value diversity. It has online resources to transform yourself, your home, your school, or your community.